EARLY MODERN LITERATURE IN HISTORY

General Editor: Cedric C. Brown
Professor of English and Head of Department, University of Reading

Within the period 1520–1740 this series discusses many kinds of writing, both within and outside the established canon. The volumes may employ different theoretical perspectives, but they share an historical awareness and an interest in seeing their texts in lively negotiation with their own and successive cultures.

Titles include:

James Loxley
ROYALISM AND POETRY IN THE ENGLISH CIVIL WARS
The Drawn Sword

Arthur F. Marotti (*editor*)
CATHOLICISM AND ANTI-CATHOLICISM IN EARLY
MODERN ENGLISH TEXTS

Mark Thornton Burnett
MASTERS AND SERVANTS IN ENGLISH RENAISSANCE
DRAMA AND CULTURE
Authority and Obedience

The series Early Modern Literature in History is published in
association with the Renaissance Texts Research Centre at the
University of Reading.

Staging Shakespeare at the New Globe

Pauline Kiernan

University of Reading
and
Shakespeare's Globe, Bankside

First published in Great Britain 1999 by
MACMILLAN PRESS LTD
Houndmills, Basingstoke, Hampshire RG21 6XS and London
Companies and representatives throughout the world

A catalogue record for this book is available from the British Library.

ISBN 0–333–66272–5 hardcover
ISBN 0–333–66273–3 paperback

First published in the United States of America 1999 by
ST. MARTIN'S PRESS, INC.,
Scholarly and Reference Division,
175 Fifth Avenue, New York, N.Y. 10010

ISBN 0–312–22274–2

Library of Congress Cataloging-in-Publication Data
Kiernan, Pauline.
Staging Shakespeare at the new Globe / Pauline Kiernan.
p.   cm. — (Early modern literature in history)
Includes bibliographical references and index.
ISBN 0–312–22274–2
1. Shakespeare, William, 1564–1616—Stage history—England–
–London.   2. Shakespeare, William, 1564–1616—Dramatic production.
3. Shakespeare, William, 1564–1616—Stage history—1950–   4. Henry
V, King of England, 1387–1422—In literature.   5. Theatre—England–
–London—History—20th century.   6. Globe Theatre (Southwark,
London, England)   7. Shakespeare, William, 1564–1616. Henry V.
I. Title.   II. Series.
PR3106.K53   1999
792.9'5'09421—dc21   98–49285
                                                              CIP

This book is printed on paper suitable for recycling and made from fully managed and sustained forest sources.

10   9   8   7   6   5   4   3
08   07   06   05   04   03   02   01   00

Printed and bound in Great Britain by
Antony Rowe Ltd, Chippenham, Wiltshire

To my mother Kathleen May Kiernan
and to the memory of
my father Thomas Patrick Kiernan

Contents

Preface

The book is divided into three parts and some explanation of its procedures is necessary. The first part is concerned with the impact of the physical conditions of the new Globe on modern theatre practices and with relating this to existing scholarship on staging in the early modern public amphitheatres. The impact of what we have discovered I have termed 'the shock of the old', but the book makes frequent reference to the work of scholars – such as J. L. Styan, Muriel Bradbrook, Bernard Beckerman, Andrew Gurr, John Orrell, Alexander Leggatt and Peter Thomson – in order to remind us that much of the existing scholarship on the subject had already suggested to us what to expect. Going back to Styan's *Shakespeare's Stagecraft* of 1967 after watching the first performances at the new Globe, one is struck by the accuracy and depth of his understanding of the effects of the physical conditions of an Elizabethan open playhouse on the performance and reception of a play.

The chapters in Part I focus on what I take to be key elements of the Globe space as they were experienced by actors and audiences in the first seasons: the implications of the spatial relationships in the physical configuration of stage and auditorium in which actors and playgoers share the same continuous light; the transformation of the audience's role; the dual perception of the actor and the role, including the impact of the boy-actor, and the ambiguities which result from a meeting of fiction- and theatre-worlds that we are not used to experiencing. There have been, at the time of writing, full-scale productions of three Shakespeare plays; one by Middleton and another by Beaumont and Fletcher, so that the findings discussed in this book are of a necessarily limited scope. But it seemed to be important to put down sooner rather than later even a partial account of what happened when plays of the early modern period first took to a reconstruction of an early modern theatre. There will be opportunities to experiment with the varieties of staging demands of different plays in the seasons ahead, and the present study represents an early sketch of the possibilities that can be discerned in the interplay of spatial relationships and dramaturgical meaning. Throughout Part I, there is an attempt to give a context for the various 'discoveries' that have been made at the new theatre by relating them to what we know of original staging conditions, to existing scholarship on the early modern theatre, and to what the plays themselves have always told us. This is followed by a chapter on the staging experiments in the new Globe's first seasons and suggests some of the possible implications for our understanding of how the original Globe stage might have been used, including such practices as '3-D' acting, the use of the balcony, diagonal blocking, and the use of different areas of the stage platform and central opening, which are re-assessed in the light of the *Henry V* staging, examined in Part II, a section which is presented as a 'chronicle' of the preparation and performance of the first production at the new Globe to be given an 'authentic' brief. This meant that the actors and director would undertake to explore certain 'authentic' production methods in an attempt to recover some original staging practices and conventions, such as doing without a 'concept' or set design, experimenting with entrances and exits, running some performances without an anachronistic fifteen-minute interval, and using clothing made from original materials. It did not include any attempt to follow what is known of original rehearsal procedures such as the practice of actors being given only their own 'parts', and the extremely short rehearsal periods. The 'chronicle' is based on the day-by-day record kept by this research fellow as academic observer throughout the whole production process (February–September 1997), from preparing the text, to the studio preparation, to rehearsals on stage, and public performances to the end of the run. Part III consists of a selection of interviews with actors and directors involved in the first three seasons. These have been kept as a separate section to facilitate reference, although it has resulted in some repetition when extracted quotations from them have been used in earlier sections of the book where to have omitted the all-important practitioner's comment on the topic being discussed at that point would have been silly.

In an attempt to make the bibliography a more useful reference tool I have included works that have not been cited in the main text.

I am aware that a book about staging at the new Globe in its first years could have taken any number of different forms. This one reflects my own theoretical and dramaturgical interests in Shakespeare and the theatre for which he wrote many of his plays, and its deliberate immediacy of response to events as they have happened, not as a process of long, considered germination and reflection. It is not part of its purpose to offer critical 'reviews' of the productions, or to defend or attack any of the artistic choices that have been made in their staging. This book reflects the hope that a reconstruction of the Globe offers an opportunity to recover something of the dynamic which existed in the theatrical space for which Shakespeare and his contemporaries wrote many of their plays so that it can invigorate live theatre today, whether in performance of plays past, present, or ones yet unknown.

P.F.K.

Acknowledgements

I would like to thank the Leverhulme Trust for its generous funding of a three-year research fellowship to study and record actor use of the new Globe, and Andrew Gurr and Cedric C. Brown at the Renaissance Texts Research Centre, University of Reading for persuading the Trust of the value of such a fellowship. I would like to thank the late Sam Wanamaker and the late Theo Crosby whose legacy is our opportunity to discover how the physical conditions of early modern staging affected the writing and performance of English drama at its most fertile phase, and to experiment with a dynamic 'new' performance space. I thank Mark Rylance and the first new Globe acting companies for welcoming an academic presence into their midst, particularly Richard Olivier, and the *Henry V* actors for invaluable interviews.

My debt to scholarship on Elizabethan and Jacobean theatres and staging practices is, of course, enormous, and the frequency of references to it in the book testifies to this. The bibliography speaks for itself as a list of acknowledgements. I have endeavoured to record acknowledgements of published criticism in notes and in the bibliography, and I apologize for any omissions.

I would also like to record my thanks to the many actors who have enriched my own understanding of Shakespeare and the processes of playing over the years, in conversations and public performances, particularly Sir Ian McKellen, Edward Petherbridge, Dame Judi Dench, Michael Gambon and the late Sir Robert Eddison. For inspiring discussions and comfort food, I thank Colin Robson and our son, Michael.

A Note on References and Abbreviations

Quotations from Shakespeare's plays are from *Shakespeare: the Complete Works*, edited by Stanley Wells and Gary Taylor (Oxford: Clarendon Press, 1986) unless otherwise stated. Quotations from *King Henry V* in Part II are from the New Cambridge Shakespeare, edited by Andrew Gurr (Cambridge: Cambridge University Press, 1992, repr. 1995).

I have silently modernized original spellings of other texts of the period. Titles of plays and books are given in full with the first citation, and in an abbreviated form thereafter. Two frequently cited books are abbreviated:

ES E. K. Chambers, *The Elizabethan Stage* (4 vols, Oxford, 1923)

WS E. K. Chambers, *William Shakespeare: a Study of Facts and Problems* (2 vols, Oxford, 1930)

All journal titles are given in full throughout.

List of Plates

Part I
The Shock of the Old

1

Introduction

This book is an account of the first years of experiment and discovery at the reconstructed Globe on Bankside, a theatre space that is such a bundle of paradoxes it defies easy categorization. It is a building that has been designed and made on Tudor principles, following historical research into sixteenth-century architecture, craftsmanship and joinery as scrupulously as modern safety regulations will allow. The building is held up by wooden pegs, constructed with green, unseasoned oak timbers, its roof is made with water-reed thatch, and its three hundred feet of wall is plastered with lime and goats' hair by means of a technique that goes back to the year 2400 BC. Actors and directors in the first seasons were describing the theatre space as 'raw', 'strange', 'exciting', 'energizing', 'dangerous', 'new', '*avant-garde*'.

The new Globe, of course, couldn't be anything other than a paradox. It's a theatre for the twenty-first century built as close as modern scholarship so far could get to the sixteenth-century original (by a nicely timed irony, the Tate Gallery of Modern Art is being installed next door in the disused Bankside Power Station). It would be strange to have no dissenting voices raised against it in an age when visual and architectural readings of the past have become heritage exercises, deadening and sanitizing what was once alive and radical. How could a reconstruction of an English oak thatched structure that was built with second-hand timbers four centuries ago be anything but a culturally barren icon for postmodernists to scoff at? Do we call it a new theatre? a new/old theatre? a Tudor-style playhouse for twentieth-century theatrical experimentation? Why an authentically built sixteenth-century structure for actors and audiences of the late second Elizabethan age anyway?

Years before Sam Wanamaker first had the idea of rebuilding the Globe, he argued that live theatre needs the unfamiliar, the frightening. He believed you could only give back the classics their frightening novelty by renewing the original stage and staging. The shock of the old first came at the new Globe during the 1995 Workshop season when actors and audiences began to discover how the physical characteristics of an early modern public amphitheatre could influence the respective roles of the actors and the playgoers in the performance space. The theatre was still a building-site; the main structure was up; the stage was temporary, made out of scaffolding and plywood, with its two huge stageposts supporting a temporary 'heavens' (the roof over the stage). There was never a full house for any of the forty-five workshops, the majority of which used texts, but the differences with those where actors did not have to read their lines, and could feel free to move, speak, gesture and experiment with direct eye-contact with a highly visible, individualized audience, showed that the theatre-space was going to offer little in the way of the familiar and the known. The opportunity afforded by the physical conditions of the space for eye contact between actor and playgoer was to become the most significant element of the transformation in the actor–audience relationship which took place when the first full-scale production was performed the following year.

The theatre's physical characteristics and the performance and reception space they create form another paradox. One hundred feet in diameter, it has 20 bays surrounding a stage that is unusually broad (44 feet wide, 25 feet deep and five feet high); the yard is nearly 80 feet in diameter, and the theatre reaches 32 feet to the top of the roof. It is open to the skies, where background noises range from helicopters and jet engines, to blasts from riverboat horns, to garrulous honking geese flying overhead. Daylight falls on everything in the space. The stage is surrounded by 1500 bodies stacked three layers high on three sides, and on one level in the balcony above the stage, who are free to move about, eat, drink and enter and leave the theatre at any point during performance time. Everyone who has experienced the space, whether actor, director, or playgoer, describes it as intimate. In my findings from the 1995 Workshop season, I wrote:

> The sense of a radically new dynamic of the Globe space is not in doubt. 'The fourth wall' – the invisible wall that cuts off the audience from actors on a proscenium stage – is an impossibility at the Globe. There is no physical or psychological dividing line between the playgoers and the players. Related to this potential change to the actor/audience relationship is the way in which the Globe space offers radical possibilities for shared experience on the part of the audience. When the yard is packed round with

standing groundlings on all sides, the audience can become an angry mob, a fearsome army, a threatening force to those on stage.[1]

In the Workshop season, when actor Mark Rylance, standing at the front of the stage, asked the groundlings to move close up against the stage, he made a mock retreat, saying: 'I suddenly feel threatened!' The audience felt that he was perhaps only half-joking. Two years later he was playing Henry V and turning the playgoers in that yard into his army urging them on to take Harfleur. In the same production, the French lords were addressing the script's insults directly at the playgoers, turning them into the 'English camp', and were greeted with jeers and hisses by 'Henry's soldiers'.

The sharing of the same light in the physical configuration of stage and auditorium at the new Globe challenges many of our modern assumptions about the playing space and the space of the audience, about acting style and the relative physical comfort of player and playgoer. A thatched roof, for example, may seem to some an impossibly quaint concession to architectural accuracy and a public relations disaster because there are no gutters to protect the groundlings in the yard. If the roof had been tiled and with a substantial gutter, there would be little danger of the playgoers in the yard getting soaked, but less chance of discovering how the presence of the groundlings in the rain speeded up performance time and gave performances a different dynamic from those played in the dry (and a surprising majority in the yard stuck it out in the rain for the complete duration in 'wet' performances).

Solving the problem of determining the theatre's orientation on the site required turning the building round, with the surprising discovery that the stage then always remained in the shade, with the sun shining into the galleries. As the new Globe's historical adviser John Orrell said, 'this was precisely the opposite of what most modern people expect; artists' impressions of the Globe commonly show its stage bathed in sunlight and its auditorium conveniently cast in the shade.' Instead of the actors being in the 'spotlight', then, it is the playgoers who are highly visible – to the actors on stage and, most significantly, to one another. The seemingly simple physical fact of the building's orientation affects every aspect of the theatre experience. If the stage is always in the shade and there is no controlled lighting to vary the focus of attention, what the audience hears often becomes more important than what it sees. Being compelled to listen closely, the playgoers then concentrate more on the story, and are compelled to 'piece out' any visual 'imperfections' with their imaginations (*Henry V*, Prologue, 23). At the new Globe, as at the old one, it would seem, there is nothing to control the audience's imagination except the story and its tellers. The daylight falling on both actor and audience alike, the proximity of the actor to the audience, the absence of stage lighting and design to direct and control the audience's attention require the actors to work harder to draw the audience into a fictitious world, but, again, paradoxically, makes it in some senses easier for the playgoers to become actively absorbed in the story. Without an elaborate set design and controlled lighting to help to do the imagining for them, the playgoers are compelled to concentrate on the voices and bodies of the actors. But the possibilities for absorbed involvement in the story mean there are also possibilities for audiences to influence performance.

It is possible to see in the experiences at the new Globe a kind of inverse paradigm of the changing circumstances of performance which sixteenth-century players and their audiences discovered when the itinerant, extemporizing traditions were brought into the fixed and comparatively enclosed space of the early modern amphitheatre. As playgoers in conventional theatres, we are used to seeing performances in a completely controlled environment. The 'lights out' in the auditorium is our cue to get ready for the presenting of a fiction played out within the two-dimensional space of a proscenium-arch stage where controlled artificial lighting will direct our gaze to focus on a predetermined set of words and actions and the characters who speak and move. The 'fourth wall' separating the audience in its darkened viewing space and the actors in their variable-lit picture frame is palpable though invisible. The audience is controlled by the physical conditions of the space unless or until it chooses to penetrate the 'fourth wall' and disrupt the performance. Take away the controlling devices of lighting, set design and props, and the relationship between actor and audience changes. The physical conditions of an open playhouse offer a means of control to both actors and audience in a shared space. Control of the circumstances of performance then becomes, to some extent, up for grabs. Audiences are free to choose to take part (in a positive or negative way) unless or until the actors stop them. When the London amphitheatres were built there was still a strong itinerant tradition of acting, one which fostered extemporization, and the opportunities for seizing on immediate possibilities for by-play with the audience so that a performance of any given play was more a 'one-off' event which that particular audience helped (or hindered?) the actors to create.

Interval-free performances go further in helping us to discover through experience how much of Shakespeare's dramaturgy has a practical basis – and why. The variation in pace, the contrasting moods, the swift scene-changes which have always been understood in terms of their dramatic effect, of course, make sense as practical necessities. Technical constraints and their opposite, invitations to exploit the architectural features of the space for dramaturgical meaning, have begun to be revealed in a new light. What we call stage directions, explicit and implicit, in Shakespeare and other dramatists who wrote for open-air playhouses seem, more than they did before, to be 'audience directions'. The traditional reason for there being so few stage directions in Shakespeare's plays, that he was on hand to 'direct' the staging, may be less important than two other factors: the aural signals within the text which have to do so much work in creating mood, establishing location and describing action; and the fixed physical structure and architectural characteristics of the stage, which present limitations to staging and blocking but also offer effective dramaturgical possibilities. A central opening, flanked by two entry doors, demands to be used not only for exit and entrance, but for concealment for eavesdropping and for discovery. Not everyone in the audience can see what is being staged within the discovery space, but if characters on stage are describing what they are seeing there, the whole house can listen and find out. Experimenting with the central opening as a discovery space has begun to offer experiential evidence for our understanding from the texts that listening can be more critical than looking. The Act Three storm in *King Lear* is presaged at the end of the preceding act in the sound effects and dialogue, so that the hearing of the distant storm and of the characters' anxious references to it come before we 'see' it, as it were. The echoing of verbal patterns and the modulating of reiterated images throughout a scene or a whole play necessarily become more pronounced and therefore of greater dramaturgical significance. Music, too, takes on a much larger role in creating and shaping mood and a sense of place and, as we have already begun to see, can offer a more expressive means of doing so than a designed set or lighting. Productions using recreated clothing of the period have begun to suggest how the dramaturgical possibilities of costume could be exploited in terms of characterization and social hierarchy, particularly in ironic potential.

From the experience of the first seasons at the new Globe it would seem that we need to find a different way of talking about the role of the audience in the performance space of the early modern theatre. Whether it is a good thing to attempt to unlearn generations-old habits of naturalistic staging and its reception, there have been the beginnings of some suggestive insights into the workings of dramatic illusion in the early modern amphitheatre space. To explore the relationship between dramaturgy and the physical structure of a theatre, particularly as it was exploited by Shakespeare, may take us beyond a limited and limiting definition of authenticity.

2
The Space of the Audience

So many of Shakespeare's established techniques – the invitation to the actor to play to the audience, the 'attacking' north-to-south entrances, the intimate soliloquy, choric speaking to the audience, the use of the aside, the grouping of characters, for liaison and repulsion – show the effort on his part to break down the barrier between actor and spectator.

Styan, *Shakespeare's Stagecraft*, 1967[1]

John Webster's description of the relationship between actor and audience is about the space which both player and playgoer inhabit:

sit in a full Theater. You will think you see so many lines drawn from the circumference of so many ears, whiles the *Actor* is the Center.

attributed to John Webster, *An Excellent Actor*, 1915[2]

What happens to the space of playing and the space of the audience when this physical configuration of the actor and audience as centre and circle is re-created, as it has been at the reconstructed Globe on Bankside, prompts re-examination of the actor–audience relationship, and a reconsideration of the question: 'Where were the boundaries of the fiction in the public amphitheatres of the early modern period?'

Webster's well-known statement makes a useful starting point for an enquiry into the question of early modern theatre 'space' because it stresses the significance of the physical relationship between player and playgoer: the actor is the centre of a circle of playgoers whose ears are the necessary receptors of what is happening on the stage. We usually talk of going to see a play; early modern playgoers talked of going to hear a play. The Prologue in *The Two Merry Milkmaids* (I.C., 1619) calls the groundlings to order: 'We hope, for your own good, you in the yard/Will lend your ears attentively to hear/Things that shall flow so smoothly to your ear...'. Jonson's Prologue in the public stage version of *The Staple of News* (1626) tells the audience they must listen to the play that is about to begin, not for the author's benefit, but for their own: 'For your own sakes, not his, he bade me say,/ Would you were come to hear, not see a play . . . hel'd have you wise./*Much rather by your ears, than by your eyes*' (emphasis added). In the Prologue Jonson wrote for the court version, the audience is told the play is being offered 'To scholars that can judge, and fair report/The sense they hear, above the vulgar sort/Of nutcrackers, that only come for sight.[3] Shakespeare's Hamlet privileges the ear above the eye when he complains of "barren spectators", the groundlings 'who are capable of nothing but inexplicable dumb-shows and noise', unlike the 'judicious' auditors who o'erweigh 'a whole theatre of others' (3.2.11–13; 26–7).

It is the actor as storyteller surrounded by an intimate circle of listening ears, rather than the actor framed inside a proscenium-arch stage being viewed by a grey outline of spectators. Baliol ('Bay') Holloway, a Shakespearean actor at the Old Vic and Stratford between the wars (Richard III, Falstaff, Othello, etc.) was asked, in the early days of the (1932) Stratford Memorial Theatre, if there was too wide a gap between the stage and stalls (the distance between an actor and the front row was often 30 feet). His reply was: 'Not really. It's like playing to Boulogne from Folkestone.' He said,

> If you come downstage on a fine night, and the visibility is good, I *have* known the front row of the stalls to be outlined in the distance.[4]

This is Middleton and Dekker, three hundred years before Holloway, describing the audience at the Fortune, which was commissioned by Henslowe and Alleyn to emulate and rival the Globe:

> Within one square a thousand heads are laid
> So close that all of heads the room seems made;
> As many faces there, filled with blithe looks,
> Show like the promising titles of new books
> Writ merrily, the readers being their own eyes,
> Which seem to move and to give plaudities;
> And here and there, whilst with obsequious ears
> Thronged heaps do listen, a cutpurse thrusts and leers
> With hawk's eyes for his prey: I need not show him,

By a hanging, villainous look yourselves may know him,
The face is drawn so rarely. Then, sir, below,
The very floor, as 'twere, waves to and fro,
And like a floating island seems to move,
Upon a sea bound in with shores above.

The Roaring Girl, 1611 (1.2.19–32)[5]

It is interesting, in the light of our experiences of the new Globe, that in this, the second scene of the play, Sir Alexander Wengrave invites his guests to 'look into my galleries', an implicit stage direction for the character to turn the stage platform and its surrounding auditorium into his sumptuous house and the playgoers into his guests. The audience is welcomed into the fiction-world to play its part, and the space of playing and the space of the audience dissolve into one.

Here is an actor in the opening season at the new Globe four hundred years after *The Roaring Girl*'s creators described an audience as a floating island:

> There is the sea of groundlings all around you. I love the unexpected and the way in which the audience *always* seems to be with you. It's like a sea – they move with you.

William Russell, 1997

With daylight falling on both players and playgoers without stage-lighting to create mood, to convey a sense of day or night, or to give specific focus to characters; without stage properties to create a sense of place, or an intricate stage design to provide a mimetic representation of a play's world, there is nothing to work on the playgoers' imagination except the story and how it is enacted by the actors.

During the Prologue season, when the first full-scale production, *The Two Gentlemen of Verona*, was mounted with the theatre still a building-site, a temporary stage area made of plywood and steel, the *frons scenae* of plywood and painted with modern materials, the huge building-crane still in residence, players and playgoers talked of a sense of radical transformation in the relationship between actor and audience. Jim Bywater, who played Launce in *The Two Gentlemen*, said that "the Globe audience shares the actor's consciousness"; Welcome Msomi, who brought his Zulu 'Macbeth',

Umabatha, to play for a week in the Opening season, talked of the 'connectedness of actors and audience' which is never lost at any point in the performance in the space; and Barrie Rutter, whose company came to put on a single performance in the Prologue season, described the experience of *A Midsummer Night*'s *Dream* as 'a party for fifteen hundred people courtesy of Will Shakespeare'. The following year, in the Opening season, when four full-scale productions (*Henry V*, *The Winter*'s *Tale*, *A Chaste Maid in Cheapside* and *The Maid*'s *Tragedy*) were mounted, it was the sense of intimacy in the space which actors were surprised at. William Russell, an experienced actor who has worked in very different theatrical spaces in a long acting career, and played the French King in *Henry V*, was struck by the different relationship between actor and audience at the Globe: 'There's this strange paradox that you feel almost a sense of shock with all those people around you, but when you go out there you have an intimacy with them which you don't have in other theatres', and David Lear, who played Glouce-ster in that play, found that the audience 'become part of what you're doing'.

The unexpected sense of intimacy which the space fosters per-haps allows us to make better sense than before of the descriptions of extreme emotional responses on the part of Elizabethan and Jacobean audiences, such as we find in John Weever's image of the relative effects of reading and hearing a work. Where the reader will weep, he wrote, the playgoer will swoon:

> If thousands flock to hear a Poet's pen,
> To hear a god, how many millions then? ...
> Wit, spend thy vigour, Poets, wits quintessense,
> *Hermes*, make great the world's eyes with tears:
> *Actors* make sighs a burden for each sentence:
> That he may sob which reads, he swound which hears.
> John Weever, *The Mirror of Martyrs*, 1601[6]

Francis Bacon famously wrote that 'the minds of men in company are more open to affections and impressions than when alone'.[7] Many descriptions of theatrical performance in the period empha-sise drama's power to affect the playgoer both physically and emotionally. We read of audiences being spell-bound or 'ravished' by characters and events on stage. Thomas Nashe's well-known description of the effect on the audiences of the 'death' of Talbot, believed to be Shakespeare's 1 *Henry VI*, is powerful testimony to the play/players' capacity to bring the whole house to tears. Talbot's bones, he writes, were 'new embalmed with the tears of ten thousand spectators at least (at several times)'.[8]

The so-called antitheatrical pamphleteers who inveighed so vehemently against the moral depravity of the evil temptress, *the theatre* (and who were often themselves failed or less than successful playwrights and were paid money by the Puritans and City Fathers to write their attacks on playing) cannot have been the most reliable of witnesses. What is interesting about their objections, though, is the emphasis placed on the theatre's affective power. Phillip Stubbes, a country schoolmaster hired by the City authorities to write pamphlets attacking the theatre, wrote:

> mark the flocking and running to theatres and curtains, daily and hourly, night and day, time and tide, to see plays and interludes; where such wanton gestures, such bawdy speeches, such laughing and fleering, such kissing and bussing, such clipping and culling, such winking and glancing of wanton eyes, and the like, is used, as is wonderful to behold. Then, these goodly pageants being done, every mate sorts to his mate, every one brings another homeward of their way very friendly, and in their secret conclaves (covertly) they play the sodomites or worse. And these be the fruits of plays and interludes for the most part.
>
> Phillip Stubbes, *The Anatomie of Abuses*, 1583[9]

Queen Elizabeth, anxious to keep the public theatres open so that the acting companies had plenty of time to rehearse their plays before her Royal Command Performances, found such objections tiresome. (Stubbes also made the mistake of publicly condemning her proposed marriage to the Duke of Alençon. Elizabeth had one of his hands cut off.)

There is some evidence to suggest that early modern playgoers might have dictated what went on in the acting-space before the players could begin to work on their imagination. Edmund Gayton writes of theatres

> where the players have been appointed, not withstanding their bills to the contrary, to act what the major part of the company had a mind to. Sometimes *Tamerlaine*, sometimes *Jugurtha* [a lost

play of about 1600], sometimes *The Jew of Malta*, and sometimes
parts of all these; and at last, none of the three taking, they were
forced to undress and put off their tragic habits, and conclude the
day with *The Merry Milkmaids*. And unless this were done and
the popular humour satisfied (as sometimes it fortuned that the
players were refractory), the benches, the tiles, the laths, the
stones, oranges, apples, nuts, flew about most liberally; and as
there were mechanics of all professions, who fell every one to his
trade, and dissolved a house in an instant, and made a ruin of a
stately fabric.

Edmund Gayton, *Pleasant Notes upon Don Quixot*, 1654[10]

Imagine going to the main house at Stratford or at the Barbican, and
booing off, say, Antony Sher, when he walks onstage as Tambur-
laine. He exits, does a quick-change, then comes on and tries again,
this time as Iago. But, no, we don't want *Othello* either. He gets sent
off for the third time by an increasingly hostile audience, changes
into another 'tragic' costume, and returns in black-garbed grief to
give us his Hamlet. This will not please us either. We tell Sher and
his company that what they *can* do is *Run For Your Wife!* (a bedroom
farce). And if Sher and his fellow actors won't do as we ask, we'll
simply smash up the joint.

The report of the demanding playgoers telling the actors which
plays they can and cannot do is unlikely to be describing a typical
scene, of course, although we have accounts of sermons being 'disrupted by jests, laughter, and the showing off of new clothes, just as
plays were'. Churchgoers who did not like the sermons that were
being preached were known to pull down preachers fom the pulpit
'or, at the very least, harrassed [them] by coughing and heckling'.[11]
Gayton's account of playhouse vandalism has been linked with the
tradition of Shrove Tuesday riots in which apprentices would attack
brothels and theatres, and the battle fought at the Cockpit with the
players in 1617, and there is the report of a Florentine visitor
describing a Venetian ambassador's visit to the theatre and encoun-
tering an audience demanding a different play from the one they
were offered.[12] Set against these examples, there is the report from
the Venetian Orazio Busino who found at the Fortune 'such a crowd
of nobility, so very well arrayed that they looked like so many
princes, listening as silently and soberly as possible'.[13] We have
evidence of lawlessness involving weapons at the open-air public
theatres, including disturbances at the Globe, but these were more

likely to be private affairs rather than a whole audience wilfully disrupting a performance. We do not know whether Globe playgoers were not at times as unresponsive to a play as 'the uncapable multitude' and 'ignorant asses' which Webster found at the premiere of *The White Devil* at the Red Bull.[14] There are plenty of references to playgoers yawning:

> the whole nest of ants... made a ring about her and their restored friend, serving instead of a dull audience of stinkards, sitting in the penny galleries of a theater, and yawning upon the players, whilst the ant began to stalk like a three-quarter sharer.[15]
> Middleton (?) *Father Hubburd's* Tale, 1604

Thomas Dekker provides another example:

> Hell being under every one of their stages, the players... might with a false Trapdoor have slipped [the devil] down, and there kept him, as a laughing stock to all their yawning spectators.
> Dekker, *Newes from Hell*, 1606[16]

Descriptions of playgoers commenting on the performance in the form of yawns or verbal interjections makes one think of the hapless Mr Wopsle in Dickens' *Great Expectations*, which I have been unable to resist quoting:

> Whenever that undecided Prince had to ask a question or state a doubt, the public helped him out with it. As for example, on the question whether 'twas nobler in the mind to suffer', some roared yes, and some no, and some inclining to both opinions, said 'toss up for it'; and quite a Debating Society arose.

The audience became more disruptive:

> On taking the recorders – very like a little black flute that had just been played in the orchestra and handed out at the door – he was called upon unanimously for Rule Britannia. When he recommended the player not to saw the air thus, the sulky man said, 'And don't *you* do it, neither; you're a deal worse than *him*!'
> But his greatest trials were in the churchyard.... I believe it is well known... that Mr Wopsle could not possibly have returned the skull, after moralizing on it, without dusting his fingers on a

white napkin taken from his breast, but even that innocent and indispensable action did not pass without the comment, 'Waiter!'

Charles Dickens, Great Expectations[17]

In the new Globe theatre-space it is impossible for the actors to ignore the expressions on the playgoers' faces. As one Workshop season director, Sean Holmes, said: 'You can see if they're yawning: You have to fight for the audience's attention'; and actor Joy Richardson who played Paulina in *The Winter's Tale* revealed: 'It's a risk making eye contact with someone in the audience. Sometimes if they're yawning, you can catch them out.' Nicholas le Prevost, who played Autolycus in *The Winter's Tale* and the King in *The Maid's Tragedy*, was not so sure you have to talk directly to the audience. 'There's an acknowledgement that takes place, it's a secret acknowledgement, but it's there, and it's real.'

Performances at the new Globe, where playgoers are free to move around the watching–listening space, to wander in and out of the theatre, to eat food and drink beer and wine sold by the hawkers during performances, have enabled us to gain a better understanding of how a highly visible, energized audience in close proximity to the actors on stage can have the potential to disrupt a performance. But it also gives us a deeper sense of the extent of the emotional effects that are possible when the actors and their story create a compelling fiction, and as a playgoer, you are free to choose whether to listen and watch. J. L. Styan's comments on the importance of the role played by the audience are particularly significant:

> Shakespeare was his own task-master, but the discipline was determined by his audience. The form and pressure of ideas and feelings in his play is their pressure on an audience. Its potential qualities of intimacy and immediacy have meaning only for a live audience. Its unity is the response of the audience.
>
> Styan, Shakespeare's Stagecraft, 1967[18]

The first performances of *The Two Gentlemen of Verona* showed how an audience which is free to move, visible to those on stage, and energized by the Globe's uniquely configured relationship between sky, building, stage and auditorium, can influence performance in ways we are not accustomed to. The actors could not have been expected to know what would happen to their production once it was exposed to a packed Globe audience that seemed, by twentieth-century theatregoing standards, intent on a raucous 'night out'. Nothing had prepared the participants for the transformation in theatregoing that took place when a Shakespeare play was performed to a packed house (audience capacity in the Prologue season averaged 94 per cent). The first preview performance of productions includes the 'penny groundlings', residents of Southwark, who pay one penny (usually £5) for a ticket in the yard around the stage. These performances so far have seen the most exuberant response from the groundlings.

One aspect of the effects of the Globe's physical conditions on the actor–audience relationship which began to emerge even in the 1995 workshop season was a sense that the 'power structure' of this relationship must have been rather different from what we are now accustomed to. If the audience in the Gayton passage was an extreme example of this, Shakespeare himself, of course, provides us with a rather more restrained version of such scenes when Theseus, for example, in *A Midsummer Night's Dream* (5.1) asks for his nuptial entertainments: 'Come now, what masques, what dances.... Is there no play/To ease the anguish of the torturing hour?' and proceeds to knock down each suggestion. He refuses 'The battle with the centaurs' with the words 'We'll none of that'; he does not want a play about the death of Orpheus, 'The riot of the tipsy baccanals/Tearing the Thracian singer in their rage', because it's an old play and he's seen it before. 'The thrice-three muses mourning for the death of learning' is, he says, not suitable for a wedding, but he will have the ten-words-long 'very tragical mirth' of Pyramus and Thisbe. Theseus, of course, is exercizing his right as a ruler to demand whatever play he likes, and Bottom and his company are inept amateur actors, but the response of the stage audience to the performance shows an arrogance shared by Berowne and the court audience in *Love's Labour's Lost* (5.2) when they heckle the hapless players of 'The Pageant of the Nine Worthies' by demanding a mimetic illusion (and showing that they know little about the workings of good drama). Criticism concerning amateur theatricals in Shakespeare's plays traditionally has tended to take the view that we are encouraged to laugh along with the stage audiences at the inept efforts of the stage actors in a straightforward identification with the 'sophisticated' spectators on stage, albeit with rather more affection. But when Costard and the actors trying to perform their Pageant to what is basically an aristocratic version of a hectoring audience, and Bottom and his company have to perform tragic events in clear hearing-distance of the snide critical commentary of Theseus and his court, the theatre audiences are encouraged towards a complex response.[19]

At one performance of *The Two Gentlemen of Verona* at the new Globe, a man in the middle gallery shouted down to the actors on the stage: 'You can't start yet, we haven't found our seats'. This real twentieth-century playgoer recalls that fictional sixteenth-century playgoer who interrupts the actor trying to do his job once the show has started:

> *Costard.* I Pompey am, –
> *Berowne.*   You lie, you are not he.
> *Costard.* I Pompey am, –

> *Love's Labour's Lost*, 5.2.542–3[20]

Before experiencing audience behaviour at the new Globe, we would have thought that an occurrence like this would have been as unlikely as a member of the audience consulting the cast list in their programme, and interrupting the first moments of a performance by shouting out: 'You're not Henry V; you're Laurence Olivier!'

The new Globe, designed as close as latest archaeological and academic scholarship can get to the original, is 100 feet in diameter. Its yard is nearly 80 feet in diameter, and the scaffold frame of the theatre rises 32 feet to the top of the roof.[21] The actor positioned away from the *frons scenae* on a 44-foot-wide stage, was/is literally at the centre of the Globe. Nearly half the audience stands in the yard that surrounds the stage platform on three sides. The 'fourth wall' – the invisible wall that cuts off the audience from the actors on a proscenium-arch stage – is not there unless actors or audience choose to erect one. Attempts to create an implied fourth wall and to act within the conventions of naturalism as in a proscenium theatre with a darkened auditorium, as if the audience is not present, can work in a small studio space, but come adrift in a space like the Globe where there is no physical or psychological dividing line between the playgoers and the players sharing the same light, and the presence of the audience is not easily ignored. In a packed house, actors on stage are surrounded by 1500 playgoers stacked on three levels (the capacity at the original Globe was about 3000). When full-scale productions at the new Globe began, it was the new empowering of the audience that struck the actors and playgoers as a revelation.

There is another paradox about the spatial relationship of actor–audience at the Globe: the stage platform is particularly large and to the playgoers, the actors look large, one imagines because they are not 'boxed-in' inside a picture-frame stage, but also because the distance between playgoer and actor is not as variable. In a Greek- or Roman-style auditorium, even if built for the same capacity as the new Globe, the playgoers would encircle the stage in low, graduated layers, not vertically stacked in galleries, so that to those in the outer 'rings' detail of expression and gesture in the actor would be less defined. At the new Globe the furthest distance between a playgoer and the centre of the stage is about 50 feet, and the playgoer can also move at any time during the performance to different parts of the watching space to get closer or for a different perspective on the action. Toby Cotterell, who played Katherine and doubled as the Boy in *Henry V*, said: 'When you are on stage, it doesn't feel big, but when you're the audience watching the play, it's a huge stage, especially when you're a groundling – when the actors come to the front of the stage they look like *giants*.'

In the 'leek scene' towards the end of *Henry V* much of the stage business involved the groundlings who were standing up against the stage. Llewellyn (David Fielder) kept beating Pistol (John McEnery) until the latter landed flat on his back on the stage, his head hanging over the edge of the stage platform right amongst the heads of the groundlings. When Llewellyn stuffed the leek into the mouth of the prone soldier, Pistol spat out the chewed pieces so that they were sprayed all over the nearest groundlings.

It is hard to use measured terms in describing the radical effects on performance and reception of the physical conditions of an Elizabethan open playhouse – actors and audience in the same light, the proximity of the actor to the audience, the absence of stage lighting and design to direct and control the audience's attention. It requires the actors to work harder to draw the audience into a fictitious world, but, again, paradoxically, makes it in some senses easier for the playgoers to become absorbed in the story. The space of the story is both the acting or storytelling space and the watching or listening space. The actors and the audience share it. Without an elaborate set design and controlled lighting to help to do the imagining for them, the playgoers are compelled to concentrate on the voices and bodies of the actors. Michael Goldman's comment on the actor–audience relationship in Shakespeare's plays is instructive here: 'The play may rise in Shakespeare's imagination and come home to our own, but it takes place between two sets of bodies, ours and the actors.'[22] The most frequent comment from actors was the need for energy to play the space, and that the energy of the playgoers – particularly the standing groundlings – generates energy on to the stage. The audience itself gives the actors energy because the Globe is pre-eminently a 'listening space'. David Lear, who played Gloucester in *Henry V*, said: 'When people are actually listening it creates a different kind of energy. The audience become part of what you're doing.'

Rylance, playing Proteus in *The Two Gentlemen of Verona*, the first production to be staged at the new Globe, thought that the playgoers were enjoying the difference from being seated in a darkened theatre looking at a proscenium arch. 'I was fortunate in having the most words to say directly to the audience and having the most opportunity to involve them directly.' Rylance found that the Globe architecture makes the experience of the playing space different: 'It is closer to pure storytelling.' All the actors on stage for that first performance with the audience remarked on the highly-charged atmosphere and the energy of the audience. Rylance thought that the audience felt free to be different: 'They weren't to be ignored. That was the biggest thing. It was as if the audience had been gagged, and were now being able to do and say what they liked.' At one performance of *Henry V*, a small group of playgoers in the yard cheered the announcement of the French dead at 4.8.72. This is a solemn moment in the play, where the text encourages the theatre audience to join Henry and his men in confronting the human cost of war and to share a sense of regret for the deaths of the enemy soldiers. A small group of playgoers could not be allowed to turn it into a jingoistic, insensitive cheapened response. Rylance, stopped in mid-speech, turned his back on the audience, and continued to read out the list of the dead in a low voice, speaking only to those on stage. The disruptive playgoers were treated as if they were despicable soldiers of Henry's army. When Rylance had came to the end of the list, he turned back to the audience, to find his disrespectful 'soldiers' now suitably chastened.

Rylance's response was rather more subtle than that of the player described in 1635 in William Davenant's epilogue to *News from Plymouth*, at the Globe, who physically threatened disruptive playgoers:

The speaker enter'd with a Sword drawn
For your own sakes (Poor Souls!) you had not best
Believe my fury was so much supprest
In'th'heat of the last Scene, as now you may
Boldly, and safely too, cry down our Play!
For you if you dare but Murmur one false Note,
In the House, or going to take Bote,
By Heav'n I'll mow you off with my long Sword,
Yeoman, and Squire, Knight, Lady and her Lord![23]
William Davenant, Epilogue,
News from Plymouth (1635)

In his first general note to the actors after the first public performance of *A Chaste Maid in Cheapside*, director Malcolm McKay said:
'because you get a lot of response from the yard, it's tempting to
play to them mostly – but there are a further one thousand sitting in
the galleries. The five hundred in the yard are not necessarily the
response of the audience as a whole. You need to bring it back
down; ground it back to reality.' Richard Olivier, director of *Henry
V*, thought that 'the relationship between the actors and the groundlings can make those in the galleries feel excluded, so it depends
how it's done; it depends on what measure of awareness it's done
on the part of the actors. In one performance, the actor was playing
so much to the groundlings – interacting with them so much that it
was actually getting in the way of the story, so that the groundlings
were enjoying the effect they were having on the actors.' The question of audience-responses was something which actors and directors discussed throughout the season. Late in the *Henry V* run,
Olivier found that 'the actors were able to pull it back to a good
measure so that there was a rapport with the groundlings that
wasn't self-indulgent, and not getting in the way of the story.'

Rylance actually stopped one performance to deal with a small
group of noisy schoolchildren in the yard who were disrupting the
show. Interestingly, this was a question of the *audience* putting the
'fourth wall' back. Toby Cockerell had mixed feelings about how far
the audience should be controlled because, he said, 'it must have
been that noise level in Shakespeare's day; a worse level, I should
think. The kids were having fun. At the time it would have been like
that: the actors would have had to find a way of engaging any of the
audience that weren't paying attention. They must have had such a
hard job.' It takes, he said, 'a different kind of actor; a different kind

of acting' to act in that kind of space to 'the kind of crowd you get at a football match'. Ben Walden, who played Bardolph and doubled as Alice in *Henry V*, suspects that playing at the new Globe is 'much more what theatre was originally intended to be'. He thinks 'a lot of the reverence that there is in modern theatres goes, and it becomes more anarchic'. The actors' testimony to the experience of playing to (with?) audiences at the new Globe recalls something of what was becoming, in Shakespeare's time, a dying tradition of interacting with the audience. When Hamlet warns the players not to speak more than is written down for them, it seems to have been a play-wright's admonition not only to the actors but to the audience, too (3.2.38–43). The experience of performance at the new Globe suggests that there may be an ironic reversal of the development from the lost tradition of extemporization to the controlled circumstances of the Elizabethan playhouse which occurred during Shakespeare's lifetime: from the highly controlled environment of a darkened auditorium, localizing sets, and mood lighting, where the perform-ance can be accurately 'pre-programmed' to the open space of uncontrollable lighting and weather, and the uncertainties of the audience's responses and provocations.

A major challenge for actors at the new Globe is to find ways for a character to make contact with the audience without losing contact with the other characters on the stage, and without stepping out of the fiction. If we can say that a production's rehearsal period takes the actors only halfway to where they will get once the audience is there, we also have to say that the playing of the play before an audience is likely to be less than half a performance if the prepara-tion in the rehearsal room does not involve the creation of a compel-ling fictional world which the characters can fully inhabit. To take such a world on to the new Globe stage and keep it whole, as it were, while inviting the audience in, requires an extremely strong preparation process, and a disciplined 'tuning' of the play once in performance. When the *Henry V* company tried out having the French lords speaking their lines in direct address to the audience in the early performances, some of the responses overwhelmed the fictional world and its characters to the extent that the story was lost. The actors had to find ways of remaining inside the fiction and bringing the audience into that world.

Scenes which encourage protagonists to draw their audiences into the world of the play are given physical support by the architecture of the open playhouse. In a scene such as 2.2 in *Cymbeline* where a taper burns in Imogen's bedroom and Iachimo, the would-be rapist, climbs out of the trunk and moves towards the sleeping woman, will audiences feel more implicated, than we usually do, as voyeuristic participants? Two of the effects of an open-air playhouse on the audience's role in this scene are that both Iachimo and the playgoers have to imagine it is dark when it is daylight. The proximity of the audience to the stage in the same ambient lighting encourages the character to invite the playgoers into a vicarious experience of what he is doing.

The implications for audience complicity in the dark deeds of characters throughout the Shakespeare canon are enormous. Richard III, Iago and Macbeth are the most obvious examples. Where they stand on the stage platform for their disclosures to the audience will have not only a direct impact on the way they are received by the audience, but also on what the audience does with this privileged knowledge when they have it. Will it be a simple matter of booing and jeering the villain? Or will audiences be persuaded by actors to develop more subtle and complex responses?

Matthew Scurfield, who played the Duke in *The Two Gentlemen*, Bedford in *Henry V*, and Yellowhammer in *A Chaste Maid*, thinks that the temptation to play out to the audience needs to be resisted. 'The story has to come first', he says. 'There is a complex narrative which needs to be respected. If you play out to the audience there's a danger of bringing them too much into the present, when you need to bring them into the presence of their imagination, where the story is taking place.'

So far, it has been the playgoers in the yard that drive the energy in this theatre space. It is significant that Jim Bywater, who played Launce in *The Two Gentlemen* talked about his experience of the space of *acting* at the Globe from the *playgoers'* point of view: 'No set – no lights – just actors! "This is obviously a story – I'm not allowed to pretend that it isn't." The audience shares the actor's consciousness.'

The first audience of *The Two Gentlemen* seemed to be performing along with the actors. Those in the yard seemed particularly conscious that they were on show. Some playgoers after the first performance said the experience was exhilarating (a significant word for such an energized audience), but that they hoped it wouldn't become like 'The Rocky Horror Show' where the audience comes ready-prepared with their responses. There were some academics and theatre critics who expressed dismay at the self-conscious rowdy responses of the groundlings. In an article in the *Independent*

Stanley Wells was quoted as saying: 'Shakespeare makes immense demands on the intellect, the imagination and the emotional response of his audiences. I find it impossible to believe that his plays were ever received in such a way'. He added: 'It is absurd to suggest that works of such complexity were written for, and popular with, audiences who misbehaved, as it is fashionable to suggest.'[24]

Throughout performances of the first production, the audience applauded after each scene, something which Drayton described in Sonnet 47 of his sequence, *Idea*:

> With those the thronged Theaters that presse,
> In the Circuit for the Lawrell strove...
> ....
> With Showts and Claps at ev'ry little pawse,
> When the proud Round on ev'ry side hath rung.
> Michael Drayton, Sonnet 47,
> *Idea*, 1594 (1619 edition)[25]

Indeed, the part performed by the audience at *The Two Gentlemen* got bigger and bigger as the season wore on – it was running to three hours and more before the season closed. This was also the case in the *Henry V* performances the following year: running time was frequently extended by 15 minutes because of the actor–audience by-play or the audience demanding to take part. Writing in 1967 nearly 30 years before a reconstructed Bankside Globe would be built, J. L. Styan said:

> It is probable that Shakespeare saw his actors as playing to their audience most of the time. In the picture-frame theatre the modern actor is withdrawn into an illusionist's setting, compelled to move from side to side of the stage (the characteristic modern stage direction is 'crosses'), playing to the other actors rather than to his audience. The Elizabethan actor was at all times vulnerable, and compelled to communicate with the audience, provoking it and provoked by it.   *Shakespeare's Stagecraft*[26]

During the first performance of *The Two Gentlemen* the play's director, Jack Shepherd, went into the actors' dressing rooms in the interval to ask them to 'calm it down' because, he said, it was getting like the Last Night of the Proms: 'The atmosphere generated by the actors and audiences was very powerful. The sharing of the play was more intense than is usual. Although the comments made by the audience were very self-conscious, often embarrassingly so, at least they were contributing, or trying to. On a good night, the "collective unconscious" was at work.' Mike Alfreds, Artistic Director of the Method & Madness Theatre Company, who came as a playgoer said, 'Initially the feeling of a lot of people in the space was exciting, but I sense there can be a danger of a sort of complacent self-indulgence on the audience's part and to treat the whole thing as a sort of jolly outing – anything goes, not really serious. There was a lot of rather inappropriate hissing and booing: I suppose audiences have to learn how to behave in the space as much as actors. Shakespeare, even at his lightest, is not pantomime.'

But how do we know the original Globe audiences did not turn moments of a play into something resembling a pantomime? It is a measure of how different from our usual playgoing experiences that we have so little with which to compare this 'joint playing' from the space of playing and from the space of the audience. 'Pantomime' is a term that seems to have been used by some commentators of performances at the new Globe because we have no other term that conveys the effects of this sense of the audience's liberation. Perhaps we need to invent a new term to describe this shared space of fictional and theatre worlds. Like the tradition of extemporizing which Shakespeare's Hamlet complained of, audience 'performing' may have been a playgoing convention that playwrights did not welcome. There is plenty of well-known evidence within the plays of the period to suggest that dramatists got disgruntled by their audience's behaviour whether it was heckling or yawning indifference. Jonson seems to have relished telling his audiences that they had no taste, that he was wasting his genius on such idiots, and he attacked fellow-playwrights and actors in the adult companies and their audiences in the so-called 'War of the Theatres', or *Poetomachia*, a quarrel that seems to have involved one or more or probably all of the following: a feud between Jonson, Marston and Dekker (whose satires on one another in their respective plays must have felt to audiences like watching a very long-running boxing tournament); an equally public slanging match between the public theatres and the private playhouses; a commercial rivalry between the Chamberlain's Men and the Admiral's Men; and a self-publicity stunt by the participating playwrights to get audiences coming back for more. David Mann has suggested that 'even Jonson's very evident quarrels with so many of his fellow practitioners need to be seen in the context of what might be called "Abuse as Entertainment",' and he adds: 'There are implications that the whole 'War of the Theatres', the so-called *Poetomachia* – poet-ver-sus-player, adult-versus-children, and poet-versus-poet – was no more than a contrivance to make money.' The Epilogue Tucca in *Satiromatrix* may ask the audience to clap because of 'this cold weather' 'but the main drift of Dekker's argument is to suggest, perhaps disingenuously, that the War is for the amusement of the audience, for 'sport'. Tucca promises that 'if you set your hands and Seals to this, Horace [meaning Jonson] will write against it, and you may have more sport.'[27] The same idea is found in *Hamlet* when Rosencrantz speaks of the players:

> *Rosencrantz.* Faith, there has been much to-do on both sides;
> and the nation holds it no sin to tar them to controversy.
> There was for a while no money bid for argument, unless the
> poet and the player went to cuffs in the question.
>
> (3.2.352–6)[28]

The particular relevance of early modern theatre's openly expressed preoccupation with itself to a study of open-playhouse audiences today is that as modern theatregoers we have had com-paratively little exposure to such frequent and explicit theatrical self-referentiality. Modern assumptions about the workings of dra-matic illusion in the plays of Shakespeare and his contemporaries tend to ignore or underestimate the precise effects of the plays' constant reminders of their status as fictional representations.[29]

Webster, when he published *The White Devil* in 1612, after it had flopped, was scathing in his resentment of the playgoers at the Red Bull on whom he thought any tragedy was wasted. The play, he said, 'wanted (that which is the only grace and setting out of a tragedy) a full and understanding auditory'.[30] Webster's statement is particu-larly significant for his view of theatre as a shared creation by play-wright, actors and audience. For Webster, the attentive, listening ears of intelligent playgoers are a prerequisite for the successful playing of a tragedy. Whether his next tragedy, *The Duchess of Malfi*, did not meet the same fate as *The White Devil* because it was given at Blackfriars and the Globe to an 'understanding auditory' (was this a pun on 'understanders' as groundlings were termed?) and not the Red Bull's 'ignorant asses', or because it was performed by the King's Men whose powers of engaging audiences with the quality of their acting are well-documented, is an intriguing question.[31] The new Globe, demonstrating that the physical conditions of an open-air playhouse require considerable powers of acting to keep a 'freewheeling' audience's attention, suggests that it was both. Serious moments at which actors were having to cope with a variety of distractions from outside the theatre (a riverboat-horn, jet-engines, and so on) could be lost on those playgoers who chose to concentrate on the distraction. Richard Olivier was aware from observing audiences that the first few times a plane flew overhead, people would look up, and then the next time it happened, would either look up again or decide to keep engaged with what was happening on the stage, so they were able 'to keep the focus through the distraction'. The physical conditions of the Globe structure work to reinforce the fiction's invitation to the audience to 'piece out our imperfections with your thoughts'. The Prologue's rhetorical question 'Can this cockpit hold the vasty fields of France?' was invariably met with an actual answer, and in the affirmative. In *The Winter's Tale* performances, playgoers would castigate Leontes for his brutal treatment of Hermione with shouts of 'shame on you!'

That the audiences in public amphitheatres indulged in participation, raucous or otherwise, does not necessarily mean playwrights wanted it to be that way, of course. Performances in early modern public ampitheatres may have been very different from what our twentieth-century sensibilities wish them to have been. Actors at the open amphitheatres were at times apparently greeted with 'mewes and hisses'[32] by their audiences. The cracking of nuts and the hissing sound of tops being taken off bottle ale, sold while the play was in performance, seem to have been the most persistent nuisances in the public theatres.[33] Sweet poesy, we are told by William Fennor, is often condemned and judged to die without just trial by a multitude 'which screwed their scurvy jaws and looked awry,/Like hissing snakes adjudging it to die'. Fennor makes a distinction between the responses of different parts of the audience, which should caution us to make generalizations about how playgoers received the plays:

> When wits of gentry did applaud the same,
> With silver shouts of high loud fame:
> Whilst understanding grounded men contemn'd it,
> And wanting wit (like fools to judge) condemn'd it.
> Clapping or hissing, is the only mean

That tries and searches out a well writ scene,
So it is thought by Ignoramus crew,
But that good wits acknowledge untrue;
The stinkards oft will hiss without a cause,
And for a bawdy jest will give applause.
                    William Fennor, *Fennors Descriptions*,
                    Epistle, 'Description of a Poet', 1616[34]

In an open-air playhouse the playgoer could choose to respond to a play that did not please, to a player he did not like, by articulating discontent. The actor could choose to interpret this otherwise:

And when he hears his play hissed, he would rather think 'bottle-Ale is opening.'
                    A Base Mercenary Poet, 1615[35]

Hissing the role, or the fiction, not the actor or playwright, is a different matter. If the playgoers are joining in the fiction, are they disrupting performance or adding to it? The term 'audience performance' gives a better sense than 'response' or 'participation' of the audience being both proactive and reactive, and goes some way towards suggesting the nature of the new relationship between the staged illusion the actors create and the extradramatic world of the playgoers which the new Globe seems to foster. But this is not an adequate term, and it will be necessary to invent a new one, which is itself a measure of the extent of the change which this relationship has undergone in the different physical conditions of the new Globe. If playgoers are hissing the characters; if the characters are 'answering' them with unwritten dialogue; where is the 'extradramatic' of this exchange? If we call it 'semi-extradramatic' to qualify the usual distinction of fictional and theatre worlds, do we mean this extemporization is somehow existing outside the fiction?

For an actor, judging how to play the stage seems possible only when the audience is there. Performance, to a quite considerable extent, cannot be 'pre-set' at the new Globe. Actors and directors found that they had to be prepared to change what was done in the rehearsal studio once they took their plays on to the stage before an audience. The actors felt that because they did not know how their production was going to work, they had to allow it to develop as the run went on. Ben Walden, who played Bardolph and Alice in *Henry V* and Tim in *A Chaste Maid*, said, 'anything that's pre-planned is likely to get shaken around a lot once it's played to the audience in that space'. Actors said that it is difficult to assess the effect of movement and voice without the presence of a full auditorium, so that staging practices such as blocking need to be worked on beyond the studio and stage rehearsal period. There are large implications, here, for some of our assumptions about the preparation of stage plays in the early modern amphitheatres. In modern theatre practices, the term 'rehearsals' usually refers to the preparation processes that take place before the play is put on before the public performances. There are normally previews which are intended to give the company the opportunity to polish the play, and a press night, and, of course, changes might be made through the run. But the usual practice is for the physical staging – the blocking, the lighting, the set and props – to be largely 'pre-set' before the 'first night', i.e. the first public performance after the previews and press night. Experiences of productions at the new Globe suggest that some processes which we normally associate with the term 'rehearsals' continue well into the play's run. Actors in *Henry V* frequently talked of how the production kept on developing in response to the space and to playing to audiences. In an important sense, then, public performances themselves could be described as 'rehearsals'. Our modern assumptions that companies in the early modern theatres had very little time to rehearse the many plays in their repertory need now to be reassessed. How the experience of preparing productions at the new Globe might relate to original rehearsal practices is explored in Chapter 4.

Actors at the new Globe distinguished between playgoers who disrupted the story and would not let them 'get on with our job', and those who wanted to take part in the telling of the story. When some commentators felt uncomfortable with the way audiences at the *Henry V* performances were booing and hissing the French, what was it that they were objecting to? When the French lords addressed the theatre audience as the enemy 'English', the actor playing the French Constable (Steven Skybell) turned to face the yard, then the galleries and up into the sky, and the allusion to the weather took on a piquant significance: 'Is not their climate foggy, raw and dull?' (3.5.16). Sun, rain, grey cloud, the joke worked whatever the playgoers saw when they looked up through the open roof. When a messenger tells the French: 'The English lie within fifteen hundred paces of your tents', the actor playing Orleans (Rory Edwards) addressed his insults to Henry's 'fat-brained followers' who were, of course, the playgoers in the yard and in the galleries: 'What a wretched and peevish fellow is this king of England, to mope with his fat-brained followers so far out of his knowledge.' The French Constable took up the insult and hurled it at the groundlings and all around the galleries so that the entire auditorium became the English camp. Cupping his hands round his mouth to create a 'loudspeaker', he bellowed: 'If the English had any apprehension they would run away.' The crowd began to boo. Some of the groundings at one performance added pieces of pizza to their verbal missiles of hisses, and at another, a middle-aged woman in the audience started pelting the 'French' with baguettes. The boos turned to growled jeers as Edwards' Orleans delivered the line that, bearing testimony to a long-surviving Anglophobic tradition, was aimed to sting: 'That they lack, for if their heads had any intellectual armour they could never wear such heavy headpieces' (3.8.112–13; 119–25).

Is this a question of 'trivializing' what the play is doing? The lines, are, after all, there. It is hard to imagine now that the original *Henry V* actors would have resisted the opportunity to work the audience in this scene. Or is our discomfort more to do with our non-Elizabethan sensibilities – a reluctance to acknowledge that the playwright was as manipulative of his audiences as this, and, apparently, getting much pleasure from whipping up such xenophobic feelings in his audience, even if the whole thing is done in a spirit of jest?

At the first public performance of *Henry V*, the empowerment of the audience and the energizing of the actors seemed to make the atmosphere doubly charged. As we have seen, the groundlings in the yard were particularly vociferous at times, especially in their responses to the French lords, who were greeted with progressively louder boos and hisses every time they came on to the stage. Actors Christian Camargo (the Dauphin), Rory Edwards (Orleans) and Craig Pinder (Rambures) were, they said, coming off-stage after the performance, completely taken aback by the audience's reaction to them. Toby Cockerell (Katherine) talked of the cheers his character received when she first came on for the French-lesson scene with Alice (3.5). She was greeted not with boos but with wolf-whistles. Henry and the English were cheered on as loudly as the French were jeered. At the first performance of *The Two Gentlemen*, Rylance as Proteus stood at one corner of the stage in front of one of the stage-posts, where the groundlings were in touching distance of the actor. It was the second scene of the second act where Julia comes to say goodbye to Proteus before he sets off, on his father's orders, for Milan. When Proteus is too embarassed to kiss Julia, after they exchange rings and she asks him if they might 'seal this bargain with a kiss' somebody in the yard shouted 'Go on, give her a kiss!', and what seemed like the rest of audience cheered him on.

When you have an audience that has felt able to join in the production as they did at *The Two Gentlemen*, hissing and booing the villain (Proteus); giving throaty, lecherous growls and wolf-whistles when the prostitute walks on (not on stage in the original script); and jeering at the sleazeball suitor and his sonnets (Thurio), what happens when the whole thing goes suddenly dark, and that same audience finds itself witnessing the enactment of an attempted rape of a woman which the men in the audience have been encouraged to find desirable? In most performances, there was a sense that the audience was suddenly being made to sober up, as it were. They were being disturbed by a change in tone before they fully registered it. The effect of this sudden turn from comfortably light-hearted comedy to potential disturbing menace suggests a more complex functioning of the ways in which comedy and tragedy could be made to work on each other in a theatre where the presence of the audience is both visible and palpable. Sudden contrasts in mood on the stage seem to be able to affect 'same-light' audiences in direct and tangible ways, a significant, and largely hitherto neglected, aspect of Shakespearean dramaturgy. It will be interesting to see the impact of the light and dark of the tragedies on this space. We have yet to see one of the major Shakespeare tragedies at the new Globe (Beaumont and Fletcher's *The Maid's Tragedy* was produced in the Opening season), but it would seem that discoveries that have been made experiencing the plays at a reconstructed open play-house suggest that the immediacy of what happens on stage, which can provoke exuberant responses in comedy, may not be comfortable for playgoers witnessing enacted violence in tragedy. The scene in which Evadne murders the King in *The Maid's Tragedy* by repeatedly stabbing him, was capable of provoking laughter, nervous and otherwise. How audiences will respond when Macduff's son is stabbed to death and when Desdemona is murdered will be instructive. When the emotional level of the audience has been carefully modulated as it is in a play like *Macbeth*, perhaps the physical horror of the actions will be emphasized because carried out under harsh daylight and given a hard edge, and therefore paradoxically more believable. How will audiences experience the sight of Juliet waking in the tomb and finding Romeo dead? or of the sound (in the remarkable acoustics of the space) of Lear's howls as he clutches the dead Cordelia to his fracturing heart? On the question of whether a tragic moment is received as theatrical melodrama or disturbing drama, it may be that we will have a better understanding of Webster's complaint about the 'uncapable multitude' which greeted *The White Devil* at the Red Bull, and his praise for the 'understanding auditory' of the *Duchess of Malfi* performances at the Blackfriars and the Globe.

Generalizations about the workings of comedy at the new Globe, like everything else to do with this theatre space, need to be resisted, but one certainty is that the relationship between actors and audience in the physical space generates a sense of fun. Direct address to an individual playgoer can make the rest of the audience feel included. A single pause can bring the house down.

At every performance of *The Two Gentlemen*, Proteus was loudly hissed and 'oo-hed and 'aa-hed' at, even when he wasn't on stage. In Act 2, Scene 7 when Julia plots her plan to join Proteus in Milan, disguised as a boy, and her maid Lucetta advises caution, the response from the audience as Julia makes her speech about the 'fire' of love that burns for her beloved, was scornful cries of 'Oooh'. The cries became almost a chorus as the scene developed and Julia offers up an eulogy of Proteus' steadfastness and loyalty. In the previous scene, Proteus has delivered one of several of his soliloquies to the audience. It is the pivotal moment when he struggles with conflicting desires: 'To leave my Julia, shall I be forsworn: To love fair Silvia, shall I be forsworn;/ To wrong my friend, I shall be much forsworn' (2.6.1–3). As he conducts this debate with himself and resolves to put his plan of betrayal into action, the audience's boos grew louder until he made his exit, and Julia enters to describe a Proteus completely at variance from the one we have just seen seconds before.

> Truer stars did govern Proteus' birth,
> His words are bounds, his oaths are oracles,
> His love sincere, his thought immaculate,
> His tears pure messengers sent from his heart,
> His heart as far from fraud as heaven from earth.

The playgoers' scorn, growing in volume with each line Julia delivered, became part of the play. This raises some questions about the nature of dramatic fiction and theatrical self-consciousness on the part of the audience. What is the relationship between the world of the play, and the world of the playgoers? It also throws up important issues about the functioning of dramatic irony in plays at the Globe. When Julia swears Proteus' loyalty she is uttering what, for her, at that moment, is the truth about him. She knows nothing of what has transpired since he arrived in Milan. She is, as her words reveal, prepared to risk great personal danger by following her love to a strange place: she knows she must travel in disguise to 'prevent/The loose encounters of lascivious men'. That she intends to give up everything for love is signalled in her generosity to her maid: 'All that is mine I leave at thy dispose,/My goods, my lands, my reputation' (2.7.40–1; 86–7). What, at this moment, is happening to the fictitious world that has been created on stage in the space of playing? Julia has to ignore the playgoers' responses to her words, has to ignore the space of the audience and go on creating the fiction even as the audience is in the process of unsettling the gap between what it knows, and what Julia knows.

In the final scene of the play the moment where Proteus asks forgiveness for his treachery and is reunited with Julia is particularly difficult to play. In rehearsals, the actors playing Proteus and Julia tried different ways of playing the ending. In early stages of rehearsal, Valentine became the central focus of the play's ending, with Proteus a notably marginalized figure standing on the edge of the platform stage. In performance, the playing of the moment changed some way through the run by public demand – literally. At the point where Valentine brings Julia and Proteus together, Proteus clasped Julia with the words: 'Bear witness, heaven, I have my wish for ever.' Julia's response through the run had been a sardonic, shrugged 'And I mine!' as she let herself be embraced (5.4.118–19). The audiences had always laughed. It was an understandable solution to the 'problem of believability' the moment poses. What, after all, is an audience supposed to feel when, having watched the painful humiliation Julia has been made to suffer, she so quickly allows a reconciliation with Proteus? At one performance, it was too much for one playgoer. As Proteus embraced Julia, a loud, clear, heartfelt voice shouted from the gallery: 'Don't do it, Julia!'

After that, Stephanie Roth, who was playing Julia, changed the way she played the scene. She felt that such a response could not be ignored. Instead of the shrug which had said, in effect 'Oh, all right, then', Julia now responded to Proteus in a way that made the reunion problematic, with an acknowledging of the pain and guilt, the humiliation and remorse that had gone before, and the attendant sense that this would not be a straightforward 'Happy Ever After' union. It became a complex, poignant moment, rather than a simplistic, comic one. (What of other 'impossible scenes' in Shakespeare? Imogen finding what she thinks is the headless corpse of her husband? Will the physical conditions of an open playhouse space help to explain why they are supposed to be 'impossible': will playgoers who know the play shout out: 'It's Cloten, Imogen! It's not Posthumous!'?)

These, then, are two examples of an audience/actor relationship at the Globe at two different moments in *The Two Gentlemen*, and together they demonstrate that labelling what happens when the space of the audience and the acting space join forces with the word 'pantomime' will not really do. Shakespeare scholar Robert Smallwood, reviewing the play in *Shakespeare Survey*, wrote of 'the audience's puerile eagerness to hiss and boo [the] stagy villainy'. Much was made of the vocal performance of the audiences at this production by the theatre critics in the national press. Michael Coveney, in his *Observer* review, described how the first-night audience 'decides that taking part is the first priority'.[36] He pointed to the potential disadvantage of such an energised, mobile, vocal audience: 'Occasionally, you feel the whole modern notion of concentration in a theatre is under threat. Passages of the play fly by unheard and unremarked, as they must have done in the early seventeenth century. Do we really want to go back to that state of affairs? To what extent do we want raucous participation at the expense of intelligent engagement?' Coveney's use of the word 'occasionally' here is worth noting, because for much of each performance most of the playgoers were interested, often absorbed, in what was happening on the stage. Immediately after jeering the French, *Henry V* audiences were silent before the kneeling Henry, his back turned on most of the audience, as they listened to his anguished railing against the price that has to be paid for the 'thrice-gorgeous ceremony' of kingship. What will happen when tragedies such as *King Lear* are played in this space may bring out new and unexpected insights into the ways in which the comic and the tragic of Shakespearean tragedy functioned in the actor–audience relationship at the Globe. What term do we use to describe *The Two Gentlemen* playgoer's powerful interjection 'Don't do it, Julia!'? Here, the response was something we have had difficulty defining because it doesn't come within our experience of modern playgoing. It was not the silence of the shocked spectator helpless to prevent a tragic ending being played out on a proscenium-arch stage; it was not the awkward, restless shuffling of a polite audience that is not quite sure how it is expected to respond; and it was clearly not 'raucous participation'. The playgoer had become so absorbed in what was happening on the stage, he was both absorbed in the fiction, and felt free to intervene from beyond the boundaries of that fiction. The implications of the effects of a shared ambient light on the emotional intensity of audience response for our understanding of the workings of dramatic illusion in early modern open playhouses is discussed in the following chapter.

One of the three plays-within-the-play in Massinger's *The Roman Actor*, which was performed by the King's Men at Blackfriars in 1626, explores this ambiguity of playgoers entering the world of the play. In Act III, Scene 2, the Empress Domitia and Emperor Domitian Caesar are the stage audience watching the inner play, *Iphis and Anaxarete*. In asides to Caesar, Domitia comments on the performance and the actors in terms of a fictional representation until the climax, when Rome's leading actor, Paris, prepares to act the suicide of Iphis. Domitia, in an equivalent of the new Globe playgoer's plea 'Don't do it, Julia!', cries out from beyond the boundaries of the inner play to become part of the fictional world. From being fully aware that she is watching a fiction, objectively describing her response to it:

> *Domitia.* Does he not act it rarely?
>   Observe with what feeling he delivers
>   His orisons to Cupid; I am rapt with't.

Domitia becomes literally enraptured by the fiction:

> *Paris*: '...As a trophy of your pride, and my affliction,
>   I'll presently hang myself.
> *Domitia*:   – Not for the world!
>   Restrain him, as you love your lives!
> *Caesar*:   Why are you
>   Transported thus, Domitia? 'tis a play.

Philip Massinger, *The Roman Actor* (III.ii), 1626

Quite a number of the higher-paying seated playgoers in the galleries at the new Globe would leave their seats to join the groundlings standing in the yard because, one imagined, they thought they would feel freer to join in. At the first performances of the Opening season, with the permanent stage in place, the atmosphere felt very much a manifestation of the feeling in the theatre of the excitement and celebratory spirit of the first public performance in a brand-new theatre, the culminating moment of a long struggle that had been finally won. The impulse on the part of the audience to take part in the event produced both deliberate and spontaneous responses. But subsequent performances suggested that the participation of the audience is simply something which the Globe space encourages. At moments when the audience is emotionally moved and goes quiet, its participation is as palpable in its still silence as in its animated noisiness.

After these first experiments on Bankside, it looks as though we will have to redefine the function of the space of Shakespeare's original audiences at the Globe, and to reconsider the role of the playgoers in the performance of plays. If an audience newly liberated, highly visible, and energized by the theatre's configuration of sky, building, stage and auditorium can influence the playing of a scene, the length of a play's running time, and make the actors feel that what is being performed is a joint creation, whose space do we call that?

3

Dramatic Illusion in the Open Playhouse

We relate to each of the figures on stage...in a number of different ways simultaneously. We relate to them as characters in a fiction, as real people moving and talking close to us, and as actors, who are at once both real and fictitious, and neither.

Michael Goldman, *Shakespeare and the Energies of Drama*, 1972[1]

FICTION AND THE VAGARIES OF PERFORMANCE CONDITIONS

During performances of *The Winter's Tale* at the new Globe, a small bundle of rags communicated with members of the audience. What appeared to be a baby's cries coming from the little parcel on the stage in prominent view of 1500 people in broad daylight would sometimes be greeted with the answering cries of real baby play-goers in the auditorium. The grown-ups could see it was not a real baby on stage, and required the persuasive skills of fine acting to compel their belief in the dramatic reality of a tiny living presence expressing the primal emotions of fear and hunger. The babies in the audience, however, simply responded to the sounds of a human adult impersonating a baby, and 'believed' it was the call of a fellow infant.

Apart from its humorous appeal, the phenomenon of the 'talking babies' in the theatre provides, I suggest, an insight into the workings of dramatic illusion in open amphitheatres. Sound can signal, even make, meaning in a particularly direct way that has to do with what *Umabatha* (the Zulu 'Macbeth') director Welcome Msomi called 'the connectedness' between actor and audience which the new Globe space fosters.

Was illusionism the norm at the original Globe? The evidence we have is, as one would expect, conflicting. Jonson's famously witty deriding of Shakespeare's cavalier attitude to the neoclassical unities

of time and place is given added force when you are standing in the
new Globe's yard listening to Time slide over 16 years and waft us
from Sicily over the seas to Bohemia. Jonson, in the folio version of
one of his plays, printed five or six years after the first performance
of *The Winter's Tale* at the Globe, tells us that he does not expect his
audiences to believe that a nation at civil war can be represented by
three rusty swords; Shakespeare, however, had always seemed to
relish fiction's power to compel belief by actually telling his audiences with mock regret, for example that he has only 'four or five
most vile and ragged foils/Right ill-disposed in brawl ridiculous' to
depict the mighty battle of Agincourt. Jonson eschews such illusionistic poverty. His plays, will not:

> purchase your delight at such a rate
> As, for it, he himself must justly hate:
> To make a child, now swaddled, to proceed
> Man, and then shoot up, in one beard, and weed,
> Past threescore years: or, with three rusty swords,
> And help of some few foot-and-half-foot words,
> Fight over York and Lancaster's long jars:
> And in the tiring-house brings wounds to scars.
> He rather prays, you will be pleas'd to see
> One such, to-day as other plays should be;
> Whether neither Chorus wafts you ore the seas;
> Nor creaking throne comes down, the boys to please;
> Nor nimble squibbe is seene, to make afear'd
> The Gentlewomen; nor roul'd bullet heard
> To say, it thunders; nor tempestuous drum
> Rumbles, to tell you when the storm doth come.
>   *Every Man in his Humour* (Folio edition, 1616)

Jonson's apparent frustration with the mimetic inadequacy of
play-acting is given a fresh significance by the experience of watching public performances at the reconstruction of the theatre where
Every Man In was performed in 1605 by the King's Men (it was
originally performed in 1598, probably at the Curtain, by the Chamberlain's Men with Shakespeare, Burbage and Kemp in the cast).
The theatre conditions offer not only a clearer understanding of
the physical constraints of attempting verisimilitude in the
playing-space of a public amphitheatre, but they also provide us

with a practical basis for examining the respective theoretical attitudes of Jonson and Shakespeare towards the functioning of fiction and drama.

Allowing for the frequent disparity between theory and practice in Jonson, it is possible to trace a fairly consistent view favouring adherence to the ideals of ancient dramatic theory. *Every Man In*, for example, shows a precise use of the stage doors to produce a strong localized effect, and in *Every Man Out of His Humour*, performed by the Chamberlain's Men at the Globe in 1599, the audience is told by two Presenters where the action is moving to, every time there is a change of locality in the play. It will be particularly valuable to see how Jonson's devices for attempting to adhere to neoclassical verisimilitude function at the new Globe. How will audiences respond to actors on the stage pointing to the tiring-house and explaining with such specificity that we have 'to presuppose the stage, the middle isle in *Paul's*; and [the tiring-house wall] the west end of it' (3.1). Of course, the effect of such efforts to compensate for the limitations of theatres to represent real buildings, real places, is that they are necessarily strongly anti-illusionistic. The pointing to the stage and tiring-house facade reinforces our sense that it is not St Paul's in a way that it doesn't when a setting remains unlocalized and we are encouraged to imagine through the fiction rather than being instructed to do so, or when locations are alluded to in the dialogue or are 'brought in with the actor', as when a character comes on stage holding keys to suggest a prison. Perhaps the discrepancies between theory and practice in Jonson will be seen to be more a direct result of his experience of finding his attempts to apply his theories resisted by the vagaries and uncertainties of the physical conditions of the open playhouse than we have been accustomed to suppose.

In the Workshop season, the Bremer Shakespeare Company, playing a scene from *As You Like It* hinted at what was to become apparent in the full-scale productions in the Opening season. 'Same-light' conditions of the performance and reception space of the Globe encourage the sense of shared fictional space. If the actor on stage looks out across the heads of the groundlings to 'see' the surrounding 'forest', and exclaims: 'Well, this is the forest of Arden!' then so it is. The forest becomes imaginatively created in the space of the playing and the space of the audience. When a full-scale production of the play was put on in 1998, there was less trust shown in the theatre's capacity to invent an imaginatively realized forest of

Arden: bare trees were hung around the galleries and placed on the stage to remind audiences that they were supposed to be in a forest (though not a very green one). From the admittedly very limited experience of using 'scenic' props to create a sense of place at the new Globe, it does seem that representational effects may do little to aid the audience's imagination. It may be that this is because such devices are conspicuously *re*-presentational on an open playhouse stage under an unfocused, unforgiving light that offers neither the self-proclaimed deception of theatrical magic 'realism' nor the carefully styled naturalism that passes itself off as 'real life'. It is difficult to find the right term to describe what kind of illusion an open playhouse fosters, and the subject merits much greater exploration, but what has been suggested so far by performances at the reconstructed Globe is an absolute requirement to trust the transforming power of the imagination. The space seems to resist attempts to provide it with much 'help' in turning it into a clearly delineated setting, whether it be a midsummer night in a wood outside Athens, a cold dawn on the vasty fields of France, the middle of the night in Brutus' orchard in ancient Rome, or midnight in a Scottish castle. Such scenes were among the subjects of the workshops in 1995, and they showed how effectively you can create a powerful sense of place on a bare stage with the characters simply being 'there' in their mind's eye, remaining inside the fiction.

Will daylight affect moments in the fiction in ways we are not used to? If actors and audience are sharing the same space, the same energy, then the kind of energy that is being generated on stage is going to strike playgoers with a raw immediacy which is not always comfortable. When Aufidius and the conspirators chant 'Kill, kill, kill, kill him!' and stab Coriolanus to death, then stand on his body in that space; when those other conspirators led by Brutus plunge their swords into the would-be Emperor; when Clarence's head is held down in the butt of malmsey and we watch him drown, when Macduff comes on stage with Macbeth's severed head; and when Gloucester's eyes are gouged out before us; the physicality of the actions will be emphasized because carried out under bright daylight, given a 'documentary' feel and make the fiction appear more 'real'. The confusion-of-fiction-and-reality effect, for example, that Kyd produces in his stage audience in *The Spanish Tragedy* when the characters attentively watch what they think are the fictional murders of members of their families in an inset play and slowly realize with growing horror that the revenge killings are not being enacted, but are real. For the actual theatre audience watching the action of the play-within-the play and its audience's response such confusion is, of course, doubled.[2] The masque of madmen at the end of Middleton's *Women Beware Women* recalls and complicates the fiction/reality confusion of the last scene of *The Spanish Tragedy*. Towards the end of *A Chaste Maid* Middleton seems to want to ram home the far-fetched suddenness of Whorehound's conversion in Act Five. His remorse seems deliberately over-cooked (he goes on and *on*), and made this playgoer, at least, long to see a staging at the new Globe of the glorious *grande guignol* effect of the end of Tourneur's *The Atheist's Tragedy* (probably played by the King's Men) when the villain D'Amville manages to knock out his own brains with the axe he was about to use on someone else:

> *Executioner*: In lifting up the axe I think h'as knock'd
>   His brains out –
> *D'Amville*:   What murderer was he
>   That lifted up my hand against my head?
> *Judge*: None but yourself my Lord.
> *D'Amville*:   I thought he was
>   A murderer that did it.
>   *The Atheist's Tragedy*, V.ii. (?) 1611[3]

Mistress Quickly's response to the play put on by Falstaff and Hal in *1 Henry IV* shows little concern with verisimilitude. In excited anticipation, she watches an actor prepare to play the part of a king: Falstaff sits on a joint-stool, puts a cushion on his head and clasps a stage-prop dagger. He calls for a cup of sack to make his 'eyes look red, that it may be thought I have wept, for I must speak in passion', and proceeds to rant in King Cambyses' vein. He pretends to be King Henry wearing a crown seated on the chair of state with the royal sceptre in his hand.

> *Hostess*: O Jesu, this is excellent sport, i'faith.
> *Falstaff*: Weep not, sweet Queen, for trickling tears are vain.
> *Hostess*: O the Father, how he holds his countenance!
> *Falstaff*: For God's sake, lords, convey my tristful Queen,
>   The tears do stop the floodgates of her eyes.

Hostess: O Jesu, he doth it as like one these harlotry players as
　　ever I see!

1 Henry IV, 2.5.394–400

Mistress Quickly is impressed because this play is just like a play.
Her response is not a spectator's submission to mimetic illusion,
where she would exclaim that the actor is just like the king; and it is
not the position argued in much metadramatic criticism of Shakespeare, that 'life too is a play'. The Hostess is comparing this player
to other players; this fiction to other fictions. Hal sees the performance and its staging as a failure, complains of what a poor imitation of life it all looks, and scoffs that the stage props will be taken
for nothing other than stage props:

> Thy state is taken for a joint-stool, thy golden sceptre for a leaden
> dagger, and thy precious rich crown for a pitiful bald crown.
>
> (2.5.383–5)[4]

Quickly is delighting in the fiction; in Falstaff acting *like an actor*.
She seems to share the effect which Tarlton was said to have on his
audiences. At one performance of a 'play of Henry the 5' at the Bull
the actor playing the Judge who was to be boxed on the ears did not
turn up, and Tarlton offered to play the Judge's part as well as his
own part of the clown. The actor playing Henry the 5

> hit Tarlton a sound box indeed, which *made the people laugh all the
> more because it was he*: but anon the Judge goes in, and immedi-
> ately Tarlton (in his clown's clothes) comes out, and asks the
> Actors what news? (saith one) hadst thou been here, thou
> shouldst have seen Prince Henry hit the Judge a terrible box on
> the ware. What man, said Tarlton, strike a Judge? It is true in
> faith, said the other. No other like, said Tarlton and it could not be
> but terrible to the Judge when the report so terrifies me, that
> methinks the blow remains still on my cheek, that it burns
> again. The people laugh at this mightily: and to this day I have
> heard it commended for rare.
>
> 'An excellent jest of Tarlton suddenly spoken'.[5]
>
> (emphasis added)

Theories of stage illusion that have been put forward over the
centuries in relation to Shakespeare's plays have been given a new

context for reappraisal by performances at the reconstructed Globe. Coleridge thought that 'We *choose* to be deceived.' He put forward his 'true Theory of Stage Illusion' where drama is

> to produce a sort of temporary half-faith, which the spectator supports by a voluntary contribution on his own part, because he knows that it is at all times in his power to see the thing as it really is.

Coleridge's more famous phrase to express this theory is 'that willing suspension of disbelief for the moment which constitutes poetic faith'.[6] For Samuel Johnson, who is too often wrongly accused of misunderstanding the workings of drama, and of condemning Shakespeare for flouting the neoclassical rules of drama, the dramatic illusion is a 'given':

> The mind revolts from evident falsehood, and fiction loses its force when it departs from the resemblance of reality. It is false that any representation is mistaken for reality; that any dramatic fable in its materiality was ever credible, or, for single moment, was ever credited. The spectators know, from the first act to the last, that the stage is only a stage, and that the players are only players.

Johnson is not suggesting that spectators will not be moved by the fiction. He wrote:

> Imitations produce pain or pleasure, not because they are mistaken for realities, but because they bring realities to mind.

His pained response to the death of Cordelia in *King Lear* which led him to half approving Nahum Tate's 'happy ending', demonstrates a strong belief that audiences can be emotionally moved by a dramatic illusion:

> I was many years ago so shocked by Cordelia's death that I know not whether I ever endured to read again the last scenes of the play till I undertook to revise them as an editor.[7]

Leonard Digges, in his poem on the death of Shakespeare, contrasts the effectiveness of Shakespeare's stage-fictions with those of Jonson. Shakespeare's plays, he says, were sell-outs; while Jonson's did not sell enough tickets to defray the costs of heating and hiring the doorkeepers:

> So I have seen, when Caesar would appear,
> And on the stage at half-sword parley were,
> Brutus and Cassius: oh how the audience
> Were ravish'd, with what wonder they went thence,
> When some new day they would not brook a line
> Of tedious (though well-laboured Catiline:
> Sejanus too was irksome, they priz'd more
> Honest Iago, or the jealous Moor.
> And though the Fox and subtle Alchemist
> Long intermitted could not quite be missed,
> Though these have sham'd all the ancients, and might raise,
> Their author's merit with a crown of bays.
> Yet these sometimes, even at a friend's desire
> Acted, have scarce defray'd the seacoal fire
> And door-keepers: when let but Falstaff come,
> Hal, Poins, the rest you scarce shall have room
> All is so pester'd: let but Beatrice
> And Benedick be seen, lo in a trice
> The Cockpit galleries, boxes, all are full.
> To hear Malvolio, that cross-garter'd gull.
> Brief, there is nothing in his wit-fraught book,
> Whose sound we would not hear, on whose worth look
> Shall pass true current to succeeding age.
>
> Prefixed to Shakespeare's *Poems*, 1640[8]

It is not surprising to learn that Digges had been a friend of Shakespeare, but his reference to the theatrical failures of Jonson's tragedies is borne out by the evidence we have. *Sejanus*, for example, flopped after its first performance in 1603, and *Catiline*, eight years later, was received with even less kindness. Digges turns Jonson's charge that Shakespeare had 'small Latin, less Greek' into a virtue: 'thou shall find he doth not borrow./One phrase from Greeks, nor Latins imitate...'.[9]

I have suggested elsewhere that at no time does a Shakespeare play ask us to see the illusion as if it were life, an argument which has been given some reinforcement by the staging of his plays at the new Globe, and at those moments when it draws our attention to its theatrical status it is not, therefore, 'disrupting' an 'illusion of reality', a point that has been made much more clear to us by experiencing the plays in a reconstructed Elizabethan amphitheatre.[10] One hopes commentators will be much less inclined to assume that a Shakespeare play is intended to be an imitation of life, an 'illusion' which, as metadramatic critics have argued, is 'broken' every time a play draws attention to itself as fiction. Where Shakespeare uses the word 'imitation' in the sense of mimetic representation, the actor is condemned for trying to present the actual physical presence of real people. Ulysses's description of Patroclus' acting also suggests that ostentatious histrionics was not the norm.

> And with ridiculous and awkward action,
> Which, slanderer, he imitation calls, –
> He pageants us. Sometime, great Agamemnon,
> Thy topless deputation he puts on;
> And like a strutting player whose conceit
> Lies in his hamstring and doth think it rich
> To hear the wooden dialogue and sound
> 'Twixt his stretch'd footing and the scaffoldage,
> Such to-be-pitied and o'er wrested seeming
> He acts thy greatness in.
>   (*Troilus and Cressida*, 1.3.149–58)

Shakespeare's other use of the word 'imitation' in the sense of mimetic illusion appears in Hamlet's advice to the players, where he speaks of actors he has seen who 'strutted and bellowed', and 'imitated humanity so abominably' (3.2.33; 35). Actors like the First Player who has the power to 'amaze indeed/The very faculty of eyes and ears' (566–7) work in fiction, not imitation:

> Is it not monstrous that this player here,
> But in a fiction, a dream of passion,
> Could force his soul so to his whole conceit
> That from her working all his visage wanned,
> Tears in his eyes, distraction in 's aspect,
> A broken voice, and his whole function suiting
> With forms to his conceit. And all for nothing,
> For Hecuba!

What's Hecuba to him, or he to Hecuba
That he should weep for her?

                            (2.2.552–61)

Fiction is used to explore realities, not imitate them; realities can only be explored with such force through fiction, a paradox which causes Hamlet so much pain.

The production of 'Pyramus and Thisbe' that is mounted in *A Midsummer Night's Dream*, including its casting and rehearsals, is one of the most explicit explorations in early modern drama of the question of mimetic illusion and the workings of fiction in drama. When Bottom starts to worry about frightening the ladies in the audience if their performances are too life-like, he suggests speaking a prologue to tell the stage audience that no one will get hurt in their play. But one anti-illusionist reassurance leads to more:

> . . . and that Pyramus is not killed indeed; and for the more better assurance, tell them that I, Pyramus, am not Pyramus, but Bottom the weaver. That will put them out of fear.
>
>   (3.1.17–19)

All the actors become preoccupied with the imagined responses of their prospective audience. Worrying that the ladies might be scared of the lion, Snout says, 'Therefore another prologue must tell he is not a lion.' On the other hand, this play of theirs must be so realistic they will need to bring moonshine into the chamber, because as Quince very reasonably explains: 'For you know, Pyramus and Thisbe meet by moonlight.' Each ridiculous suggestion for staging the play is shown to be prompted by the actors' assumption that their audience will believe that Bottom is Pyramus, and that Pyramus really does stab himself to death with a sword on the stage; that Snug is actually a lion, Snout really a wall. At one point, Snout and Bottom take the illusionist view of drama to such an extreme, they paradoxically (and, by now, logically), want to eliminate illusion altogether, and make the play more than life-like: they want to be able to dispense with the notion of drama being 'like' life, and be real life, and use a real moon for moonshine. Possibly the biggest joke about drama's relations with illusion is that the rehearsal 'room' for the 'Pyramus and Thisbe' players is, of course, not a room at all. Before they start to rehearse they pointedly refer to their surroundings.

Pat, pat; and here's a marvellous place for our play.
This green plot shall be our stage, this
Hawthorn-brake our tiring- house...
(3.1.2–4)

The actors are rehearsing in a green plot, which they are pretending
is a stage, which is supposed to represent a green plot in the fiction.
For the *Dream* audience, of course, there is a further layer of irony:
within this fiction, real actors are playing actors on the actual stage
before us. The fictional actors are pretending the stage is a green plot,
pretending the green plot is a stage, which is meant to represent a
green plot where the lovers in their fiction meet. The force of the
irony here is given its full weight when the same light is falling on the
theatre audience, the actors playing the stage audience, and the
actors playing the actors in the play which the stage audience is
watching. Theseus is watching Snout playing Thisbe, and we, of
course, are watching Theseus, a character who doesn't know he's in
a play, who believes he is about to marry the Queen of the Amazons,
and that his home is in Athens, as opposed to the fictional representation of a fictitious Ovidian myth he is watching. When all this is
apprehended by the *Dream*'s real audience sharing the same atmo-
spheric and lighting conditions in the intimate space of an open-air
circular playhouse, the effect is unlike the experience of watching in a
darkened auditorium with the spotlight on the figures on stage. The
simple physical fact that the sky above and the light that comes from
it are there means that a play exploring the illusion and reality
becomes much more complex in the mind and feelings of the playgoer. The physical conditions of the performance and reception
space, as it were, make meaning too. Instead of talking in terms of
the interplay of text, interpretative performance, and audience
response, we have now to speak of another element: the physical
conditions of performance and reception of the space of playing and
the space of the audience.

THE ACTOR OR THE ROLE?

He's not counted a gentleman that knows not
Dick Burbage and Will Kemp.'
Kemp, as he is made to say in *The Second Part of*
The Return from Parnassus, IV, iii. 41–2. 1603 (?)

Performances at the new Globe have offered some opportunity to readdress questions about the relationship between the fiction and theatre worlds in the public amphitheatres of Shakespeare's time. When the *Henry V* cast made their first entrance on the stage, an entrance staggered and in pairs, to take up their drumming positions at all points of the stage and look out at the auditorium, they prompted the question, Who are they? The characters they will be playing in the play proper? Or the actors who have come to the theatre that day to do their job? At the start of this *Henry V* performance, it was hard to say. The actors were not in full costume – they came on stage bare-headed in undershirts and hose and bearing drums and staves. The distinction between role and actor is blurred at the end of the show when the actors came back on stage to perform their drumming again. Katherine and Henry had exited through the central opening, a shower of confetti drifting from the trap in the heavens, to be followed by the Chorus delivering the Epilogue. The cast came back on stage. This time, the male actors playing Katherine, the French Queen and Alice were wearing the dresses we had just seen them in, but without their head-dresses. Henry was no longer wearing his crown. Every character/actor had taken off some item of his costume. They started beating the stage floor with their staves in a variation on the jig tradition. Again, this prompted the question: Are they half in, half out of character? half in; half out of the fiction? It was an interesting moment. Each figure on the stage was simultaneously both actor and role. The effect, though it was not part of the scripted play, had something in common with that of the dual awareness in the audience of role and player that is prompted by inductions to Elizabethan and Jacobean plays such as we find in Jonson:

> Now gentlemen, I go
> To turn an actor, and a humorist,
> Where, ere I do resume my present person,
> We hope to make the circles of your eyes
> Flow with distilled laughter.
> > *Every Man In His Humour*, 1598; 1605

Plays with Inductions which confuse actors and playgoers include Webster's well-known Induction specially written for the Globe's adult version of Marston's *The Malcontent* (1604), a play that had been staged at the indoor Blackfriars by the boys' company. In the

Induction to the play performed in the outdoor Globe, five members of the Globe company, actors Will Sly, Richard Burbage, John Lowin, John Sinklo and Henry Condell, and the tireman, or, wardrobe-keeper, take part under their own names. Two of them, disguised as 'gallants' in the audience, try to sit on the stage (a practice which would have been allowed to important spectators of the boys' version in the indoor theatre) and are told by the Tireman to get off:

> *Tireman*: Sir, the gentlemen will be angry if you sit here.
> *Sly*: Why? we may sit upon the stage at the private house.
> > *The Malcontent*, 1604. Induction

Sly (as actor or as role?) then parodies the ostentatious posturing of the hall theatre gallant, and refuses to get off the stage. He is, he says, 'one that hath seen this play often, and can give them intelligence for their action'. The 'gallant' (it's worth noting again here, that the question of using quote marks round the word itself reflects the difficulty of categorising actor–role/role–role in this Induction) is offering to *direct* the play, and perhaps the most significant aspect of Webster's exploration of actor–role–audience relationships is that what is being presented is a *playgoer* telling the players what to do. Such an intrusion and infringement of the performance space was clearly not to be tolerated by the Globe actors. A few years later, in 1607, Francis Beaumont's Induction to *The Knight of the Burning Pestle*, written for the Children of the Queen's Revels company at the Blackfriars indoor playhouse, has a player pretending to be a playgoer citizen (a Grocer) who gets up on to the stage to angrily protest against the Prologue's snide references to civic pride and values and the social distance between court and city and to demand that the actors perform a play for popular tastes. The Grocer interrupts the Prologue in what seems to be a fictionalized, indoor playhouse version of the behaviour of Gayton's playgoers at outdoor theatres we looked at in Chapter 2:

> Why could you not be contented with 'The Legend of Whittington', or 'The Life and Death of Sir Thomas Gresham, with 'The Building of the Royal', or 'The Story of Queen Eleanor, with the rearing of London Bridge upon Woolsacks'?
> > Francis Beaumont, *The Knight of the Burning Pestle*, 1607.
> > Induction

Beaumont's play is frequently self-referential. The boy players are not only made to burlesque the behaviour of citizen playgoers in the private playhouses but to allude to their own beauty. A child playing the Wife says at one point, 'Sirrah, didst thou ever see a prettier child? How it behaves itself, I warrant ye, and speaks, and looks, and perts up the head?' (1.i.94–5). Beaumont's play was itself a parody of Thomas Heywood's *Four Prentices of London*, in which a grocer and his wife, in the audience, insist that their apprentice Ralph shall have a part in the play on stage. The practice of including the representation of players in their fictions reflects the playwrights' interest in dramatic self-reference, and, it is reasonable to suppose, audiences' enjoyment of their dual awareness of actor and role.

One contemporary description of an actor suggests that audiences would have been well aware of the distinction between acting and posturing, inhabiting a role and displaying one:

> When he doth hold conference upon the stage; and should look directly in his fellows face; he turns about his voice into the assembly for applause-sake, like a Trumpeter in the fields, that shifts places to get an echo.
>
> J. Cocke, 'A Common Player', 1615[11]

Like Shakespeare's 'strutting player' who listens to the conversation between his ham-strung legs and the wooden boards of the stage platform, this actor draws attention to his performance, not to the role or the fiction he is supposed to be creating. He is not engaging with his fellow-actors on the stage, but stepping out of the fiction so that the audience may play its part in applauding a solo turn. This is not drama.

If we look at two contemporary descriptions of an actor who was renowned for engaging the emotions of the audience, we seem to have contradictory views on whether it is the actor or the role that the audience perceives:

> Mine host was full of ale and history; Why, he could tell
> The inch where Richmond stood, where Richard fell:
> Besides what of his knowledge he could say,
> He had authentic notice from the play;
> Which I might guess, by's must'ring up the ghosts,
> And policies, not incident to hosts;

But chiefly by that one perspicuous thing,
Where he mistook a player for a king.
For when he would have said, King Richard died,
And call'd – A horse! a horse! – he, Burbage cried.
    Iter Boreale c.1618. Poems of Richard Corbet.[12]

In another allusion, the same actor is perceived as the role alone, so compellingly that even the other actors on the stage submit to his power:

He's gone and with him what a world are dead!
Which he reviv'd, to be revived so,
No more young Hamlet, old Hieronymo
King Lear, the grieved Moor, and more beside,
That lived in him; have now forever died,
Oft have I seen him, leap into a grave
Suiting the person which he seem'd to have
Of a sad lover, with so true an eye
That there I would have sworn he meant to die;
Oft have I seen play this part in jest,
So lively, that spectators, and the rest
Of his sad crew, whilst he did but seem'd to bleed
Amazed, thought even then he died indeed.
A Funeral Elegy on the Death of the famous Actor Richard Burbage who died on Saturday in Lent the 13th of March 1618[13]

Thomas Heywood wrote of the spectator 'wrapt in contemplation, as if the performer were the man personated' (significantly, the term 'personation' was coined in the 1590s to describe what actors do); and in his famous description of the actor's powers of moving an audience to tears, Thomas Nashe wrote:

How would it have joyed brave Talbot (the terror of the French) to think that after he had lain two hundred years in his tomb, he should triumph again on the stage, and have his bones new embalmed with the tears of ten thousand spectators at least (at several times), who in the Tragedian that represents his person, imagine they behold him fresh bleeding.
        Thomas Nashe, *Pierce Penniless*, 1592[14]

Performances so far at the new Globe have begun to offer up further insights into the ways in which illusionistic modes of drama developed in the early modern period. Experience of public performances in its first two years suggests that the transition from the extemporizing which foregrounded the gap between the actor and the role to the illusionistic performance which effected to narrow or close that gap was a more complex and less complete process than is indicated by referring to it as a broadly 'comedy-to-tragedy' development. If the clown's stand-up comic routine was going out of fashion even before the 1590s, the audience's perception of the actor behind the role, on which the humour of his extradramatic addresses so depended, may have continued strongly alongside the emerging fashion for a self-contained dramatic illusion. In Shakespeare's plays there are the numerous examples of self-referential allusions we can identify (and who knows how many we have not), ranging from the explicit call to audience recollection in Hamlet (Burbage)'s line reminding Polonius of another play they have just starred in. Polonius says: 'I did enact Julius Caesar. I was killed i'th' Capitol. Brutus killed me.' Hamlet-Burbage-Brutus recalls his own part in the killing: 'It was a brute part of him to kill so capital a calf there' (*Julius Caesar*, 3.2.99–102), to the self-referential immediacy (to the fiction, the role, the gender-role, and the actor) of Cleopatra's.

> The quick comedians will stage us, and present
> Our Alexandrian revels. Antony
> Shall be brought drunken forth, and I shall see
> Some squeaking Cleopatra boy my greatness
> I'th' posture of a whore.
> (*Antony and Cleopatra*, 5.2.212–17)

The vivid description of extemporizing clowning, written in a play that was entered on the Stationers' Register in 1608, suggests that if the clown act had died out, it was still alive in audience's memories. As with many other aspects of staging, we seem to be learning that the practices and changes in the actor–role relationship in the early modern theatre are even less clear-cut than we thought.

At a student performance of *Periander* (1607/8) at Oxford, a student actor pretended to be a member of the audience, and hissed at the Prologue: 'Pox: begin your play, and leave your prating.' The real audience was well and truly 'had', because as a witness reported, 'as soon as it once appeared that he was an actor their disdain and anger turned to much pleasure and content'.[15] In Barrie Rutter's production of *A Midsummer Night's Dream* which came to the new Globe in 1996 for a single performance, the first half was played in the actors' own clothes – mostly jeans and T-shirts. Rutter had warned the audience before the play began that three cases of costumes had been lost somewhere between Rio and Heathrow, so that as with their rapid acclimatizing to the stage and space, the players had to improvize to make up for the loss of any help from costume in their characterization – no mean feat when you are a 14-stone actor pretending to be a workman transformed into a fairy with nothing but movement and voice to disguise you. When Rutter walked on stage for the second half, dressed in a black coat festooned with rainbow-coloured favours, a splendid hat covered in flowers and sprouting tall, winking pheasant feathers, the audience – in the yard and in the galleries alike – gave a roar of applause. The irony of course was now that Rutter was dressed in character, it was not Oberon the playgoers were applauding, but the actor who had had to play the part not dressed for it throughout the first half, as well as the costume itself. It provided another example of the blurring of boundaries between the world of the play and the world of the playgoers.

For the style of acting we're used to in the late twentieth century we use terms like 'naturalistic', 'psychologically real' in which the actor fuses player and role into a seamless 'one', when it's good acting; and 'artificially contrived', 'over-the-top' or plain 'ham', when it's bad. But Elizabethan and Stuart theatre audiences seem to have had a more complex and sophisticated apprehension of the relationship between actor and role.

William E. Gruber has argued that Shakespeare's audience had no difficulty in seeing how an actor 'can simultaneously be "in" and "out" of character'. He writes:

> Renaissance commentators, when they describe their reactions to histrionic performance, frequently indicate an awareness simultaneously of the character and of the actor's degree of impersonation or metamorphosis. This awareness by no means distances them critically from the performance. Even when they describe empathic responses (what one would nowadays call

'identifications') to a character, Tudor and Stuart theatre-goers – unlike modern audiences – not only tolerate visible contradictions between actor and role, but apparently they consider them to be the affective basis of spectating.[16]

Gruber's insistence on what he calls the 'affective strategy' of the dissonances between actor and character is important. An audience's simultaneous awareness of real actor and assumed role is a dual perspective. When Coriolanus says, 'Like a dull actor now/I have forgot my part, and I am out...' (*Coriolanus* 5.3.40–1), we are not suddenly taken out of the fictional world to contemplate only the *actor* Alan Howard or the *actor* Ian McKellen. As with the dissonances between the dramatic and the real world, we are conscious of both the role and the actor. Before the interval in *A Chaste Maid in Cheapside* the long 'childbed' scene (III.ii) in which Mistress Allwit displays her latest baby to an assortment of Puritan women is brought to an end in this production with a rousing rendition of 'Shall we gather at the river?' as the characters paraded off stage and through the yard. One of the Puritan women, Mistress Jugg (Bill Stewart), remained on the stage all alone, carried away with her singing. She suddenly became aware of the audience, and rushed off the stage in embarassment to join the parade. In the moment when the singing stopped, it was the character's recognition of the extradramatic world of the audience which was being signalled by the interplay between the role, Mistress Jugg, and the actor behind her. When the extradramatic world exists in the same light as that of the dramatic world, it seems paradoxically to reinforce our perception of the fiction. 'The body of the actor', Goldman writes, 'works against the abstractness of his art', and the audience relates to figures on the stage 'as characters in a fiction, as real people moving and talking close to us, and as actors, who are at once both real and fictitious, and neither.'[17]

William Kemp's practice of sharing a joke with his audience against other characters on the stage was echoed in the 'tennis balls' scene in *Henry V* performances at the new Globe, when King Henry, seated on his throne in the authority position in front of the central opening, would encourage the audience to support him in his confrontation with the French ambassador with a slight movement of the head. When Henry stood up and dextrously juggled three of the balls in the air to turn the gesture of humiliation on its head the playgoers cheered.

THE BOY-ACTOR

The boy-actor on the Elizabethan and Jacobean stage has been the subject of much academic criticism of the drama of the period in the last twenty years.[18] Before London's public theatres were closed by Puritan edict in 1642 'play-boys' disguised as girls disguised as boys appeared in at least seventy-five plays by nearly forty different playwrights.'[19]

> He who is most womanish and best resembles the female sex, gives best content. The more criminous, the more applauded is he; and by how much more obscene he is, the more skilful he is accounted. What cannot he persuade who is such a one? meretrocious, effeminate and lust-provoking fashions of...apparel'
>
> Prynne, *Histrio-Mastix* (1633)

Studies have focused on what is perceived to have been the homoeroticism of the boy-actor in the original staging of the plays when women were forbidden from acting on a public stage in England (also the case in the Netherlands and parts of Protestant Germany). From the experience of seeing a young man in the part of Katherine in *Henry V*, it would seem that some recent scholarship's emphasis on homoerotic effects on the original audiences (apparently taking its cue from certain antitheatrical pamphleteers of the period who railed against the provocative effects on male playgoers of boys dressed up as women on the public stage) may have to be reassessed. Toby Cockerell's Katherine demonstrated that, as with any aspect of the power of fiction in drama to compel belief, it is possible for audiences to accept that what is before them on stage is a young woman, unless there are potentially self-reflexive allusions to the boy-actor behind the costume within the play (as when Isabel, the French Queen, says in 5.2: 'Happily a woman's voice may do some good/When articles too nicely urged be stood on'). Even then, the allusion cannot be said to have 'disrupted' the audience's concentration on the story. The question of whether Katherine is played by a male actor or a female actor seems to become an irrelevance. Cockerell himself was surprised that some playgoers didn't know Katherine was being played by a man. It seems that the audiences simply believed 'Katherine' was a young woman, as original audiences watching boy-actors playing women seem to have done:

In the last few days the King's Players have been here. They acted with enormous applause to full houses...They had tragedies (too) which they acted with skill and decorum and in which some things, both speech and action, brought forth tears. – Moreover, the famous Desdemona killed before us by her husband, although she always acted her whole part supremely well, yet when she was killed she was even more moving, for when she fell back upon the bed she implored the pity of the spectators by her very face.

> Henry Jackson, 1610; trans. William Fulman in 1660, from a letter in Corpus Christi Library (Ms ccc 304ff 83v and 84r)

The testimonies of playgoers in the period such as Thomas Platter, George Sandys, Thomas Coryat and Lady Mary Wroth suggest that audiences simply accepted boys in women's clothes as a dramatic convention.[20] The question of what it is the playgoers see – the female character or the boy behind the dress – seems to become redundant much of the time. Malcolm McKay, *Chaste Maid* director, said, 'We wanted to avoid audiences saying,' Oh it's another man dressed up as a woman.' *Damon and Pythias*, a play of around 1565 by Richard Edwards about male friendship, written in rhyme, and a probable source for Shakespeare's *Two Gentlemen of Verona*, which was put on for a single performance as part of the Prologue season in 1996, had an all-female cast dressed as 1950s Teddy boys to give a twentieth-century take on the practice of casting boys in female roles. Re-casting the all-male play into an all-female one was made more intriguing by having the two main leads wear kilts, as Scottish tourists in Syracuse, the cross-dressing thereby becoming a double-cross dressing: women pretending to be men by dressing up in skirts was an ingenious touch. The cross-dressing for *Damon* was not, of course, a true parallel to the boy actors playing female roles in sixteeth-century English drama where there are both male and female characters (or to the play's original cast of boys playing men, for that matter). The complexities and ambiguities of sexual identity and gender roles which Shakespeare's mature comedies explore – *As You Like It* and *Twelfth Night*, for example – have a quite different effect on audiences. With *Damon* the effect of female actors dressing up as men was a straightforward comic device.

DOUBLING

Productions in the new Globe opening season revealed differing approaches to the practice of doubling. Actors in *Henry V* were encouraged to try not to worry about whether the audience would 'recognise' a doubled part. Original Globe audiences would have not been bothered and, as we have seen, there is plenty of evidence within the plays to suggest that playgoers enjoyed, even relished, the ambiguities inherent in doubling. The 1997 audiences seemed particularly pleased with the symmetry in the doubling of the English traitors and the French lords in *Henry V*. Actor Christian Camargo took an interesting doubling route (which involved a change of national identity, a gender and a biological sex-change which enabled him to effect the miraculous metamorphosis of becoming his own mother), playing first the English conspirator, Sir Thomas Gray (2.2), then the French heir, the Dauphin (2.4; 3.6; 3.8; 4.2; 4.5);[21] and finally, Isabel, Queen of France, mother of the Dauphin (5.2). In a discussion of the representation of the professional players in Elizabethan plays, David Mann makes the important point that 'When an actor doubles, it affects his relations with each role, with the audience, with the text and with the stage event', and he adds: 'Doubling was intimately bound up with a special complicity of the audience in the action of the Elizabethan theatre, which was inherent in the physical space that it occupied.... The Elizabethan player could not, as in a proscenium-arch theatre, begin his business without establishing an accommodation with the audience.'[22] As even the lightest doubling exercise will reveal, whatever the intended theatre space, much fun can be derived from 'ironic' doubling. Audiences at *Henry V* performances seemed to find the (a)symmetry in Llwellyn and Le Fer doubled by David Fielder particularly satisfying when it came to the moment in 5.1. when Llwellyn beats up Pistol, after watching Fielder as Le Fer beaten up by Pistol in 4.4.

As we have seen, Toby Cockerell doubled the parts of the French Princess Katherine and the Boy, which offered important insights into the use of sexual disguise in Shakespeare. For *A Chaste Maid in Cheapside*, five female actors joined the *Henry V* actors, although some male actors were cast as female characters as well. Mature male actors playing women in broad comedy, of course, would not be expected to provide new discoveries.

For the production of *The Winter's Tale*, director David Freeman felt it was important to disguise the doubling of parts as much as possible, and some of the decisions on staging took this into account. The actors playing Hermione, Leontes, Paulina, Antigonus, Dion and Cliomenes doubled as shepherds; Anna-Livia Ryan doubled the parts of brother and sister, Mamillius and Perdita; and Nicholas le Prevost doubled as Autolycus and Time.

'OR ELSE THE PUCK A LIAR CALL'

When Puck tells us at the end of *A Midsummer Night's Dream* to think that we have but dreamed all that we have just seen, it is one of those moments in Shakespearean drama when a play draws attention to its fictitious status, and to the actor behind the role. He challenges the audience to call him a liar. Knowing that since we've all been engrossed for the past two-and-a-half hours in the actions and emotions of a King and Queen of the Fairies, a legendary hero called Theseus and the Queen of the Amazons, we're going to look pretty silly if we do say he's a liar. And that's not to mention the group of workmen in the play-within-the-play, putting on a show – Pyramus and Thisbe – based on a fiction from the myths of Ovid, *and* constantly reminding their audience that they're not really who they say they are, but actors playing fictional roles: Bottom, you remember, actually steps out of his role – steps out of the *play* at one point to address the Pyramus and Thisbe audience after he talks to Wall who is played by Snout:

> *Bottom as Pyramus*: Thou wall, O wall, O sweet and lovely wall,
>   Show me thy chink, to blink through with mine eye.
>   (*Wall shows his chink*)
>   Thanks, courteous wall, Jove shields thee well for this.
>   But what see I? No Thisbe do I see.
>   O wicked wall, through whom I see no bliss.
>   Cursed be thy stones for thus deceiving me.

At this point Theseus jokes:

> The wall, methinks, being sensible, should curse again.

Bottom stops the performance, and turns to Theseus.

No, in truth sir, he should not. 'Deceiving me' is Thisbe's cue. She is to enter now, and I am to spy her through the wall. You shall see, it will fall pat as I told you.

> *Enter Flute as Thisbe*
> Yonder she comes.
> (5.1.173–87)

When the play is finished, of course, Pyramus even rises from the dead to interrupt Theseus and ask if the audience would now like an epilogue or a bergamask dance. Theseus cannot take any more amateur theatricals ('No epilogue, I pray you; for your play needs no excuse. Never excuse; for when the players are all dead there need none to be blamed', 349–51). No epilogue to this tragedy, but there is a dance. One staging tradition which has yet to be revived at the reconstructed Globe is, of course, a post-tragedy jig. The implications for our understanding of the relationships between fiction and theatre worlds, the interplay of real and 'feigned' passion in the early modern theatre by experiencing the effects of a bawdy song and dance number replacing the corpses on the stage after the closing scenes of *Hamlet*, *Othello* and *King Lear*, promise to be considerable.

4

Dramaturgy, 3-D Staging and Daylight Space

Shakespeare's scenes were written to be acted in depth and staged in three dimensions.

J. L. Styan, *Shakespeare's Stagecraft*[1]

ORIENTEERING

One important practical question which quickly emerged once performances began at the new Globe was to do with terminology for the physical dimensions of the space. There is no 'front' and 'back' in a circle. Terms for theatrical space that we are accustomed to using do not work in a playhouse where the audience encircles the stage. If you say 'front of the stage', what part are you talking about? Can we use the phrase, 'facing the audience'? You cannot *face* 360 degrees. Who are you facing? The playgoers in the gentleman's rooms abutting the tiring-house wall? The ones in the Lords' rooms above the stage? The groundlings and seated playgoers on the north-east of the stage, which we are predisposed to describe as the front? We can no longer speak of actors 'facing the yard' because the groundlings are on three sides of the stage. Ben Walden, who played Speed in *The Two Gentlemen*, Bardolph and Alice in *Henry V* and Tim in *A Chaste Maid*, said that after two seasons playing in the space, 'I still think I don't do enough to embrace the very back of the audience. . . . There is a tendency to get in front of the pillars out front, but that 'out front' is right the way behind you. It's a circular space, so that there is no "out front" here, and you have to remember to play all the circle.' The terms 'downstage' and 'upstage' (originally used in theatres where the stage was raked) will still just about do for the new Globe, although a new terminology will probably need to be found, preferably one that will evolve as actors get used to the space. Over the first three seasons, I have tried different methods of 'orienteering', such as using compass points – north, south, east and west of the theatre's historical orientation which is about 48 degrees east of true north – but that seems impossibly cumbersome, and have been tempted to go back to an early idea, prompted by the experience of watching the 45 workshops in the 1995 season, when, trying to find ways of describing the 'gentlemen's rooms' on the middle gallery on either side of the tiring-house façade, the image of a clock emerged. The 'gentlemen's rooms' would become 10 to 2 and 10 past 2, with the lords' rooms between them at 12 o'clock; and the rest of the auditory circle would go round the clock in ten-minute intervals. Those directly 'facing' the stage would be 6 o'clock, and so on. But this is too unsatisfactory, because it assumes a reference point of view suited to a picture-frame stage. All of this was rejected as inadequate, but the exercise did provide a useful demonstration of the necessity of 're-orienteering' our terminology for an open-air arena.

Before the archive video cameras were installed so that we could film performances at the new Globe for research purposes, the problem presented itself again. A conventional position such as the middle gallery directly facing the stage would do little to accommodate the spatial relations of the stage: to show, for example, the breadth and depth possibilities for groupings, the use of the stage pillars for concealment and eavesdropping, and would give little visual indication of the presence of the playgoers and therefore their importance in the performance experience. It was decided to install three cameras in an attempt to do justice to the group dynamics: one was placed in the top gallery from the side of the stage looking across the stage; another, quite far round, stage left of centre which gives a 'lozenge' shape to the shots and gives a sense of the depth and breadth of the stage and some coverage of the audience; and the third, which is closer to the conventional angle facing the stage, but positioned slightly stage right of centre. Only by recording performance from three different angles was it possible to give some idea of the complex workings of the stage. It was still necessary to make use of a 'roving' fourth camera to record the playgoers' responses.

In the Workshop season, playgoers with seat tickets headed straight for what they thought would be the best seats in the house – in the lower gallery facing the stage, or facing south-west. These seats are, of course, furthest from the stage. The implications of the assumption that facing the stage means you see and hear everything better seem to have had a considerable effect on how the actors played the space, but this effect itself was compounded by how the actors came on to the stage: they tended to head straight for the front of the stage. As Sir Peter Hall demonstrated in his *Julius Caesar* workshop when he deliberately walked in a straight line from the central opening to the edge of the stage platform, the impulse of the modern actor is to move to the 'front' of the stage, and showed us the need for actors to remember to play to the sides of the stage by 'pulling' the players back and across from the front of the stage with an imaginary 'rope'. The difficulty with the findings in the early performances at the new Globe on this aspect of the stage plan is that it led to a circular argument: do actors head for the 'front' of the stage because of their twentieth-century training? Do playgoers head for the lower gallery 'facing-stage' position because of their twentieth-century 'training'?

As we have seen, it became quickly apparent in the Workshop season that the physical characteristics of the Globe provide a different kind of acting and playgoing space from the dynamic produced by open-air promenade or any variation on the darkened-auditorium/proscenium arch that we have experienced in modern times. Even actors who have considerable experience of acting among the audience, encouraging audience participation and so on, felt that it was completely different. In the Workshop season, the Bremer Shakespeare Company, who tour Europe specializing in daylight performance with no scenery and sets and using very physical playing and staging, thought that the space presented a different kind of challenge. Performing 50 to 60 performances a year, they are used to playing theatre spaces they have never been to before, constantly confronted, as they say, with the challenges of new, strange and often troublesome spaces. Even these actors, who with their experience of the quick-change pace of multiple casting with only a few actors, drawing the audiences on to the stage and pushing the stage out into the audience, said that the Globe space made the actor feel vulnerable and, together with many of the actors in other workshops, felt this was part of why the space was exciting. As we have seen, in the following seasons, when full-length plays were performed to much larger audiences with a crowded yard, the dynamic of the space was, not surprisingly, noticeably more complex. The energy of the playgoers, their close and visible proximity to the actors, and sense of the shared experiencing of a story, were held in dynamic tension with the potential danger of spontaneity, the uncertainties of playgoers' responses, a sense that anything might happen to disrupt the scripted performance.

BLOCKING AND 3-D ACTING

Some of the things that were learned from the Prologue season confirmed what had already been discovered in the Workshop season. We saw again the need for actors to play to the sides of the stage and to the middle and upper galleries and to resist using the pillars as a 'proscenium-arch' frame. Diagonal blocking, using the depth as well as the breadth of the stage, makes for effective staging; almost continuous movement is required in this space, with long speeches delivered by static actors to be avoided, although rare moments of stillness for specific dramatic effect can have double the impact (as long as the actor is not stuck to a pillar and thereby invisible to some of the audience).

Actors found that working the corners of the stage, on the extreme edges outside the pillars were powerful positions to play, and 'hot' spots for interacting with the playgoers. Here, the actor is in touch with the audience in direct and tangible ways. The pillar has the effect of separating the corner spot from the rest of the stage. It is a natural place from which to deliver a soliloquy and and other methods of direct address to the audience. In dialogue, or when the character is listening or watching, the stage corner is also a powerful position. Even when the actor has turned into the stage to interact with other characters, the audience is 'with' him or her. This is an important discovery for dramaturgical positioning on the stage – a character automatically has the audience on his or her 'side', unless there is a compelling reason for the audience's hostility to the character. Even this qualification will need to be tested further, however. Does the power of this position itself extend to encouraging audiences to empathize with a character whose actions are morally reprehensible? What will happen when Richard of Gloucester stands at the corner of the stage to let us in on his plans to murder his way to the throne? How much will the dramaturgical possibilities of the physical proximity of actor and playgoer in shared light contribute to the audience's sense of complicity?

The 'authority' position on the stage is under the 'fiery cloud' on the Heavens trap, in the middle of the stage-width, forward of the *frons*, and back from the pillars. It is this spot at which all the playgoers' sightlines converge and thus offers the least obstruction from the stage pillars. The sides of the stage on all three galleries have excellent sightlines when the actor is positioned here. But it does depend on the way that any given moment or scene is staged and blocked. The physical architecture of the theatre with its same-light conditions, emphasizing as it does the importance of the configuration of actor and audience, can 'direct' the playing of the space.

The least successful moments on this stage have been when actors line up in a 'proscenium-arch' frame at the 'front' of the stage, playing to the main crowd in the yard, or when delivering a long speech standing still. It does look as though it may take some time to know how to work the Globe stage to its full advantage. *The Maid's Tragedy* was an interesting example of how the use of long diagonals can work to create effective '3-D' acting (although the Masque in this production was staged two-dimensionally). When the stage is crowded with figures, as it was to spectacular effect in *Umabatha*, the visiting Zulu 'Macbeth' that played for a week in the Opening season, the space offered up unexpected visual possibilities for stunning patterns and shapes. Blocking in this production was more 'proscenium-arch' style but in scenes where many figures were moving on stage, the *effect* for playgoers at the sides of the stage was more three-dimensional. This was something that was strongly evident in the Workshop season in Phillip Stafford's 'swordfighting' sessions which created more dynamic spectacles and were most effectively experienced by playgoers in the galleries at the sides of the stage and in the Lords' rooms above the stage. When the stage is crowded with figures wielding swords in battle, playgoers 'facing' the stage see a group of undifferentiated movements, a 'messy' effect; while those at the sides are given a more delineated, 'clean-lined' shape.

Gaynor McFarlane who directed the *Damon and Pythias* production, put on for a single performance in the Prologue season, felt strongly that the actors needed to get some idea of the physical space of the new Globe before they started to rehearse in the warehouse rehearsal room. On the first day of their two-and-a-half week rehearsal period, the company explored the different parts of the theatre like a reconnaissance party. The actors took up positions in different parts of the empty theatre: in the top gallery, in the yard, in the middle gallery and on the stage. Actors standing at the extreme side of the top gallery, right next to the *frons scenae*, called down to those on stage to start speaking, and were amazed at how well they could hear the words of the speakers on the stage, and how close the stage felt. It was a valuable exercise in discovering the paradox of the Globe space: a 100-foot diameter with an unusually broad stage, open to the elements and the sounds of man-made flying engines, feels like a small, enclosed and intimate world.

It is difficult to generalize about actor-use of this space. Some actors embraced it as if it was an old friend, and relished playing to the whole surround of playgoers; others seemed wary of exploiting the new (old) staging possibilities offered by its size and shape, although every one of the players said they found the experience of the audience response exhilarating. Many actors thought it was difficult to judge voice and audibility and found themselves shouting at first, when they discovered that what was needed was greater definition and clarity, not volume, something which actors in the full-length productions playing to much larger audiences were particularly conscious of discovering as the seasons wore on, and discussed at greater length later in the chapter.

There were 45 public workshop sessions over five weeks in the 1995 season. Actors and directors who volunteered their services and time were offered the opportunity to explore the space in virtually any way they wished. Some took advantage of the chance to explore a public open-air playhouse; a good many used the workshop more as a rehearsal period for a current production in preparation so that little was learnt about the Globe space; and some, like young director Sean Holmes and his actors, embraced the theatre as a radical space of theatrical experimentation.

An understandable assumption was that the theatre would require the actor to play and speak 'big'. But what emerged was that movement, gesture and voice do not need to be on the grand scale. Sue Lefton, Movement Coach for the four productions in the Opening season, said that at the new Globe, 'you have to give clarity to the movement, to give it shape, colour and plasticity. The space responds to strong definition. Basically it encourages a movement that culminates in a larger physical expression: if the actor is unspecific it shows in an unfocused space, open to the air, without controlled lighting.'

One of the most important lessons learnt about blocking on the Globe stage is that two characters talking to each other need to have a certain distance between them. Too close together, and the exchange becomes unfocused, the audience made disengaged with the characters' interaction. Paradoxically, two people facing each other on a long and deep diagonal can create a dynamic, intimate tension in the space between them which has the effect of bringing them closer together emotionally and psychologically, and of drawing the audience into the moment.

REHEARSALS

The kind of blocking in which long diagonals are paradoxically conducive to intimate dialogue, where physical closeness of two actors is usually a blocking norm, is an example of how modern preparation practices in a relatively small, enclosed rehearsal space require some adjustment for productions in a reconstructed open playhouse. Similarly, in the modern rehearsal space, the instinct of the actor delivering a soliloquy would usually mean standing at the 'front' of the stage at the centre. As we have seen, at the new Globe, it is one of the two corner edges of the stage, or the 'authority' position just before the *frons scenae* that offer the most effective spots for soliloquies. These are two of the more obvious examples of the ways in which the working-out of blocking and movement extends the 'rehearsal' process beyond the previews and press 'night' and into the run of the production in public performance. Two points have to made when conjecturing comparisons between rehearsals at the original Globe and those at the new. Firstly, modern theatre practices tend to favour rehearsal periods which allow time for as much textual and character analysis as possible, including improvisation work, voice classes, movement classes, historical and background research when the play is not contemporary, and various other preparation techniques and processes which individual directors may like to explore with the acting company. In the case of the new Globe companies, five weeks are spent inside the rehearsal studio, one week on the stage for technicals, and about one-and-a-half weeks for previews and press 'nights' before the 'first night' of the run proper. It is important to keep these figures in mind when considering the second point which relates to the traditional view of original Globe companies having what is seen as such little time for rehearsing the plays in their repertory system. If we use the information to be gleaned from Henslowe's *Diary*, which forms the detailed records of the dramatic company that was the main rival to that of Shakespeare, where it shows that a new play was usually added to the company's repertory every three weeks, and that the period between the arrival of a new play script and its first public performance was about three weeks, it quickly becomes clear that, if we were to compare like with like, the relative rehearsal 'capacity' of the old and new Globe companies may not be so dissimilar. Such a view is necessarily conjectural, but perhaps not so implausible. If we look again at the rehearsal practices of the new Globe companies we might allow that voice and movement classes, for example, were not a priority in the original Globe company, or that extensive discussion and analysis of the text was not needed when the language of a play was in common currency, and anno-tated editions, glossaries and dictionaries of sexual puns were not required, and when the writer himself was there to help out any of the actors with a particular nuance of meaning, and who would also, of course, be available to offer instant character notes for every member of the cast. Historical and background research into Eliza-bethan and Jacobean England would not, one presumes, require reading social history books when the actors themselves were living it, although they may have wanted some instruction on ancient Rome or the Battle of Agincourt. The original players would not have been given a copy of the entire script (it would have been too costly and time-consuming to write out fifteen or so copies of the play), but only their 'part' or 'parts' if they were doubling. Even allowing for every member of the the cast being able to find an opportunity to read the company's play script, it would have had to be read *in situ* – no constant re-reading of your own personal copy at home, in the tavern, and not on the bus or tube on the way to work, of course. The original players also had the advantage of the playwright's instructions and suggestions for staging; modern actors need time to work out some of the most basic staging when there are few stage directions. Three weeks' rehearsal time now begins to seem less of a high-speed operation when it is put into the perspective of the number of processes that are required to reconstruct the plays in the present day.

So far, the comparison has been between single productions, that is to say, not in repertory. What happens when a new Globe com-pany begins rehearsals for its second production of the season while performances of the first are being given needs to be examined. After *Henry V* had been running for a week, the company began rehearsals for *A Chaste Maid*. The schedule meant that the actors gave one performance of *Henry V* every day and rehearsed *A Chaste*

Maid every day, Tuesdays to Sundays. There were no rehearsals for *Henry V* once the public run began. After allowing for modern theatre working-practices for lunch-and supper-breaks and so on, there remained a substantial part of each working day for rehearsing *A Chaste Maid*. Again, the assumption that play rehearsals in Shakespeare's Globe were a rushed, *ad hoc* affair that would not allow time for detailed attention to dramaturgical meaning and staging seems less tenable. A German visitor to England, Johannes Rheinanus, provided some telling evidence in 1611 for the care and preparation that went into productions in the early modern period:

> So far as the actors are concerned they, as I have noticed in England, are daily instructed, as it were in a school, so that even the most eminent actors have to allow themselves to be taught their places by the dramatists, and this gives life and ornament to a well-written play, so that it is no wonder that the English players (I speak of skilled ones) surpass others and have the advantage over them.[2]

It would seem that our twentieth-century rehearsal practices have encouraged a significant underestimating of the amount of work on a play that could be achieved in three weeks by a company of highly experienced professional actors who have worked with one another as a very successful company on a great number of plays in the same theatre space and are used to open playhouse audiences.

When, five weeks into the rehearsal period the Prologue season company moved their *Two Gentlemen* on to the stage, some actors made the point that it took some time to learn how to fill the space at first. Rebecca Lenkiewicz said: 'The stage seemed big, much much bigger than the rehearsal space despite accurate mark-ups. The first run-through felt as if one would topple off the stage. The space felt a bit jagged with no real "focus" that you have with the usual proscenium-arch stage. It wasn't a nice space to play without the audience. But once full, the experience was transformed and it felt as though the stage and house itself were completely filled with the actions of the actors.' Stephanie Roth, who played Julia, said that 'choices made in the rehearsal room had to become more focused, specific and energized once you got on stage'. She also made the point that moving from the rehearsal room into the theatre was, for her, 'very freeing. It felt like a breath of fresh air', and that learning to fill the space – 'to fill each corner of that stage' was 'a great challenge'. The

Globe's Artistic Director Mark Rylance, who played Proteus, thought that 'pre-programming' performance was particularly unsuited to the Globe space.

Barrie Rutter's Northern Broadsides production of *A Midsummer Night's Dream* arrived at the Globe just after finishing a tour of Brazil, spent two hours' rehearsing on the stage in front of an audience of builders and pleasantly surprised tourists, and less than an hour later, the company were putting on their single performance to a packed Globe house. The company discovered how to exploit many of the space's possibilities. Even within the few hours of rehearsal time, actors were moving through the auditorium to test acoustics and sightlines, and the rehearsal audience were brought into the exercise to play a major role. Rutter would shout to a punter in the upper gallery: 'Can you hear that?'; actors on the stage would try out lines to see how to embrace the whole auditorium. If something didn't work – a blocking move, an exit, an entrance – Rutter would experiment to find other ways to play the scene. The public rehearsal of this *Dream* was probably an object-lesson in how a company of actors can find out how to get used to the Globe space in a very short time. The Northern Broadsides company had toured this production in all kinds of spaces – from purpose-built theatres to factories. Asked whether he felt his approach to the rehearsal process would need to be any different from his usual approach – would you want, for example, actors to spend more time getting used to the space, the distinctive configuration of audience/actor of the new Globe? Rutter replied: 'No and No – as we proved with just two hours' familiarization, then a party for fifteen hundred people courtesy of Will Shakespeare.' From the experience of the *Dream* performance, one theatre critic suggested that the new Globe would benefit from being a theatre for visiting productions.

For *The Winter's Tale*, Production Director David Freeman encouraged the actors from early on in the rehearsal period to conceptualize a fictive, timeless world and to prepare to use the Globe structure as a place of ritual. The staging involved creating an invented world inspired by African and Asian cultures, suggesting the recycling of the débris of twentieth-century objects: a layer of red earth covered the whole of the stage floor, on top of which sat large items of furniture such as sandbags and huge tractor tyres, with one cut in half and stuck together in inverted crescent shapes to form a throne and placed in front of the stage-right pillar for the second act, and inside the stage-left pillar for the fifth act. The placing of the throne determined much of the blocking in these acts: if action is played out in front of a pillar or in the 'line' between the two pillars for any length of time sightline problems are created for many of the playgoers. Localizing was 'colour-coded': red for Sicily, dark blue for Bohemia, and the overall use of the stage was strongly localized, with items of furniture indicating different playing areas. For the second scene of Act 2 it was decided to designate the area in front of the stage-left entry-door as 'the prison' where the audience is introduced to Paulina (Joy Richardson) when she tries to visit the imprisoned Hermione, and is told that the Queen has been prematurely delivered of a daughter. The staging of the exits and entrances of the gaoler and Emilia meant that Paulina had her back to a large part of the audience throughout. With the scene's primary focus invisible to two-thirds of the audience it seemed as if the 'fourth wall' between actor and audience had been put back.

Blocking for this production was determined to an extent by the production's emphasis on the actors' creation and involvement in a mythic, other world. It was predominantly close to the ground – actors sat on cushions or squatted a lot of the time. This scrupulous commitment to inhabiting a strictly delimited dramatic world within the confines of the stage platform prompts some interesting questions about the functioning of dramatic illusion on the amphitheatre stages of the early modern period. It would seem to offer another paradox about the relationship between dramatic and theatrical worlds at the new Globe. In a conventional proscenium-arch theatre, the world that is usually created for us by the performers within the picture frame, and presented to us as a naturalistic mimetic illusion is intended, or is likely, to encourage a Coleridgean suspension of disbelief. The more successful the actors are in inhabiting their roles and the world of the play, the more the audience will be engaged with that fiction. This is probably why so much recent metadramatic criticism has confused metadramatic moments in Shakespeare's plays with what has been termed 'sabotaging' the illusion that the audience is meant to believe it is watching 'real life'. James Calderwood's argument, for example, that *Hamlet*'s 'instances of theatricalization in Denmark serve as Brechtian alienating devices to shatter our illusion of Danish reality and cut the cord of our imaginative life there' may be true for audiences in a darkened auditorium watching a performance of exemplary verisimilitude, but is clearly not the experience of playgoers at an outdoor theatre on Bankside at the turn of the sixteenth century or the twentieth.[3]

When *The Maid's Tragedy* was taken from the rehearsal space on to the Globe stage much of the blocking was changed. Director Lucy Bailey made use of long diagonals and angles in the blocking, and found that intimate scenes worked well in the space upstage before the *frons*. For the scene towards the end of the play in which Evadne kills the king, the royal bed was positioned in the centre of the stage. When Evadne tied the King's arms to the bedposts and proceeded to repeatedly stab him, the effect of the daylight and the audience's proximity to the action made the response more problematic, I would think, than if the scene had been staged under controlled lighting and played to a darkened auditorium. The stark proximity and immediacy of what might otherwise have been seen at a safe detachment from the more stylized 'picture' within a proscenium arch will most certainly affect the playing and reception of violent scenes in other plays of the early modern period: *Titus Andronicus*, *The Revenger's Tragedy* and *King Lear* being just three among those that come immediately to mind. Moments which provoke the kind of shock that has nervous laughter threatening to break out of the horror will create, I am sure, a more complex sense of unease in the audience.

LOCATION SETTING

The early modern amphitheatre's unlocalized stage worked to provoke the audience's imagination and their participation in creating 'place' or location. The imaginative creation of onstage forests, prisons, studies and tombs in the minds of the playgoers played a substantial part in producing the dramaturgical significance of a particular locale, what might be called creating something out of nothing. Shakespeare's stage has no life-like trees or grassy banks to represent the Forest of Arden, no magical lighting to creative a midsummer night in a forest, no high-tech rainmakers to whip up a storm on a heath for Lear or a tempest at Prospero's bidding; they exist only in the language of the play and the minds of the actors and their audience. With little or no attempt to achieve a mimetic verisimilitude the greater is the opportunity for 'place' to be invested with significances beyond its mere physical existence. We are accustomed to talking of Shakespeare's 'psychological realism' in terms of his techniques of characterization; but perhaps we need also to examine the psychological dimension of his 'landscape', the countries of his characters' minds that the audience is invited to enter without explicit physical signposts. When Henry and his lords in the *Henry V* production at the new Globe stood on stage and looked out to the yard to address the rest of the English army, Agincourt became paradoxically more 'real' as a psychological state experienced by soldiers dreading the coming of the dawn on the eve of battle because the place had to be created out of no-thing, that is to say, no physical substantial representation of a battlefield. Words, music, the players' passion and the audience's imagination proved potent creators of the scene's meaning with a bare stage and a packed auditorium.

Alan Dessen has reminded us that there was no Elizabethan equivalent for 'offstage' or 'onstage', and argues for the need to recover the lost theatrical vocabulary of the plays of the period. Dessen makes the important observation that in Elizabethan staging, the mind-set of stage directions is 'actor- centred'. The Elizabethan audience, he says, expected the environment to come in with the actor, signalled by his costume or by hand-held props.[4] At the new Globe, Eastcheap tavern was signalled by a barrel, a few beer tankards and Mistress Quickly's landlady's apron; the royal courts of England and of France by their respective chairs of state; Harfleur by the balcony, the *frons scenae* and the central opening.

CREATING NIGHT

One of the great comic moments during the rehearsal scenes for 'Pyramus and Thisbe' in *A Midsummer Night's Dream* has been when the actors discuss the staging problems of night scenes.

> *Snout*: Doth the moon shine the night we play our play?
> *Bottom*: A Calendar, a calendar! Look in the almanac; find out moonshine, find out moonshine.
> *Quince*: Yes, it doth shine that night.
> *Bottom*: Why, then may you leave a casement of the great chamber   window, where we play, open; and the moon may shine in at   the casement. (3.1.48–54)

Bottom and his company are preparing their play for an indoor theatre space, the 'great chamber' of Theseus' palace. The original actors at The Theatre, Shoreditch and the Globe performed *A Midsummer Night's Dream* in an open amphitheatre in afternoon

daylight. The technical problem of representing night and moonlight is a question the Chamberlain's Men were also having to
solve. It is another of the many layers of irony at work in this use
of the play-within-a-play, that the *Dream* audience is given an
explicit demonstration of the fictitiousness of drama. Starveling
walks on stage to present the person of Moonshine, and says:
'This lantern doth the horned moon present./ Myself the man
in'th'moon do seem to be.' His literal-minded audience loudly
protests that if the lantern is the moon, and Starveling is the
man in the moon, then Starveling should be inside the lantern.
Starveling, who at least understands the way dramatic illusion
works better than his audience, even if he does fail in the execution,
says:

> All I have to say is to tell you that the lantern is the moon, I the
> man i'th'moon, this thorn bush my thorn bush, and this my dog
> my dog.   (5.1.252–4)

Starveling seems to know that the audience has to bring its imagination into play, but does not realize the actor has to provide the
stimulus that is required for the process to begin. It is how you tell
the story, not whether it is true, that compels belief.

On an unbearably hot noon in the middle of May 1997 inside the
top floor of a Victorian warehouse in Southwark the *Henry V* company began to create the battle of Agincourt. A dozen or so men,
dressed in long white linen shirts, woollen hose and flat leather
shoes, moved cautiously about the straw-strewn floor blindfolded,
feeling their way from 'camp to camp', where 'Fire answers fire,
and through their play flames/Each battle sees the other's umber'd
face'. Creating night was one of the exercises the cast of *Henry V*
would be performing during a rehearsal process which focused to a
great extent on preparing for the physical conditions of the playing
space of the new Globe. It was decided not to use lanterns or other
equivalents of original devices of carried lights to denote the night
scenes before the battle of Agincourt. The English soldiers wrapped
blankets round their tired, aching bodies and looked toward the
rising light on the 'horizon' to compel the audience's belief in the
turning of night into dawn.

INTIMATE SCENES

As long as actors are facing each other and not parallel, the audience can be drawn into quiet, intimate scenes. The upper-gallery extreme side-bays are surprisingly good for love scenes/confrontation scenes. Peter McEnery and Peter Egan playing the quarrel scene from *Julius Caesar* (4.2) in the Workshop season provided almost a test case in how a long duologue can be made to work for all parts of the house. The scene is a characteristically Shakespearean exercise in exquisite modulation of feeling, and it plays best 'on its feet'. Witnessing, in the same continuous light, the tension between the two men, the rise and fall of emotion seemed to become more strongly defined than when the actors are seated under controlled lighting: the sense of violent threat alternating with the petulant squabbling of a lovers' tiff ('*Cassius*: I denied you not. *Brutus*: Yes you did') and concluding with a reconciliation in an embrace. The playing of the scene showed that it is not necessary to turn to the Globe audience to include them in the dynamic taking place between two actors; that natural speaking can range from quiet tenderness to anger/frustration/even violence if the voice is focused; and that gestures do not need to be large to communicate themselves to the upper galleries. Like the most effective use of voice in this theatre – which is clarity rather than volume – effective use of gesture seems to rely more on strength, precision, *meaning* it, rather than sweeping gestures or dramatic arm movements.

Another understandable assumption was that internalized acting would be difficult, if not impossible, in this space. One of the surprises as a playgoer is to find yourself absorbed in an intimate moment, not only when you're standing a few inches away from the actors on stage, but when you are sitting high up in the top gallery next to the tiring-house wall, feeling that you are 'there', right where the emotion is being felt. Intimate scenes work very well upstage in front of the *frons*. Patrick Godfrey, who played the Old Shepherd in *The Winter's Tale* and Calianax in *The Maid's Tragedy*, said, 'You are drawn towards the front of the stage all the time but as an actor you feel you are making better contact by moving downstage. I suspect that the really powerful place is to be up by the back wall . . .'.

SIGNALLING THE START

At the original open amphitheatres, the use of three 'soundings' (offstage knocks) would be used to signal the start of performance.

Jonson liked to incorporate this practice into his scripts. His *Every Man Out of His Humour*, performed by Shakespeare's company at the Globe in 1599, begins with the stage direction '*After the second sounding. Enter* Cordatus, Asper and Mitis' and over three hundred lines later, '*The third sounding*' at which the Prologue enters. There are then another eighty-odd lines before the Act I, Scene 1 begins.

For the first full-length production at the new Globe, experiments with traditional soundings were felt to be ineffective because it was difficult to make the knocks on the tiring-house wall heard by the whole audience. It was decided to have two stage-hands enter from the flanking doors on to the stage to beat a large gong three times. For *A Chaste Maid* characters came on to perform a jig-like dance which suggested a 'story' of how the two young lovers in the play came to meet. The start of *The Maid's Tragedy* was signalled when musicians took up positions among the playgoers, in different parts and at different levels of the auditorium, playing a brass fanfare. (At the original open amphitheatres, a trumpeter on a platform next to the hut on top of the stage-cover would alert playgoers that the performance would begin.) *The Winters' Tale* began with a ceremonial *tableau vivant* prologue accompanied by music, lasting five minutes in which the Sicilian court prepares for Polixenes' departure by bestowing him with gifts. It was felt by all the companies that testing out different signalling-the-start and warming-up-the-audience practices will be an interesting ongoing process of experiment and discovery.

USE OF ARCHITECTURAL FEATURES OF THE STAGE

The Stage Pillars

The most controversial feature of the new Globe has been the stage pillars. The mock-up stage built for the Workshop season was built from modern steel scaffolding, clad in plywood without decoration or modelling, and the prototype stage pillars were sited 5ft 6in. from the 'front' and 5ft 6 in. from the sides of the stage and were 3ft square at their base. Some of the workshop actors and directors wanted to dispense with the pillars altogether; others suggested that they should be placed 12ft 6in. or so back from the 'front' of the stage and 9ft 6in. or so in from the sides of the stage. The general objection was that they affected the way things were staged, which, of course it could be argued, is what the reconstructed theatre has been built for. We do not have detailed evidence about stage pillars in early modern amphitheatres, but allusions within the plays, the visual records, and the technical requirements of Elizabethan building practices suggest that the pillars were integral to the structure. After a period of debate between actors, academics, architects and builders, it was decided to increase the cantilever from 5ft 6in. to 8ft 3in. which moved the columns closer together (from being 33 feet apart down to 27ft 6in. apart) as well as further from the stage edges. This reduced the height of the stage roof, and called for a 'penthouse' extension to which guttering could be attached. The new position of the columns on the temporary Prologue-season stage was kept for the final version. The flanking doors were shifted slightly further apart. The question of the stage pillars still provokes different reactions from actors and directors.

Gaynor McFarlane, director of *Damon and Pythias* in the Prologue season said: 'It never occurred to me that the pillars would be a handicap. I thought that they might offer interesting opportunities for actors to create and define a particular acting space, and to hide, eavesdrop or just lean. The positioning of the pillars was helpful in providing an entrance or exit to the side doors, an idea of journeying or a place from which to share confidences with the audience.' Nicholas le Prevost, who played Autolycus in *The Winter's Tale* and the King in *The Maid's Tragedy* in the Opening season thought the stage needed a larger frontstage area that is free: 'the pillars need to go back six feet!'

The pillars present potential sightline problems for some parts of a performance. Vincent Brimble, Mistress Quickly and Gower in *Henry V*, and Mistress Fork in *A Chaste Maid*, thought you have to keep things 'very loosely blocked so you can move around, and you should never stay in one place too long if you possibly can, so that you're masked for as little time as possible'.

Blocking on the new Globe stage needs to be dynamic, then, for several reasons. The pillars have to be brought into dynamic relationship with the blocking so that no actor is concealed from any playgoer for more than a second or so. The pillars, as well as having an important practical use for actors' positionings on the stage, make effective places for concealment and eavesdropping as early modern playtexts have suggested. But more importantly, perhaps, and rather more difficult to define, the mere fact of their physical presence lends an authority to the playing space. One of the hottest hot spots, as we have seen, is the extreme corners of the stage outside the pillars. The pillars offer effective means of defining spatial relations between interacting groups of characters on the stage. In *The Two Gentlemen* production, Valentine was hidden behind one of the pillars as his friend Proteus attempted to rape Sylvia.

The Central Opening

We have yet to see a clown poke his head through the curtains of the central opening at the new Globe, as Tarlton is known to have done. The dramaturgical significances of who enters through which door are likely to enrich any given scene's meaning as we suspect they did at early modern theatres.

So far, experience of using the central opening as a discovery space has proved problematic because a large part of the audience and playgoers in the lords' rooms above the stage cannot see what is happening in the space. It may be that audiences will need to be given more practice in listening skills before the central opening can be used effectively as it must have been at the original Globe. For the 'statue' scene in *The Winter's Tale*, the company experimented with different positions, and it was decided against placing Hermione in the discovery space as the original staging would have done, largely a result of poor sightlines for some of the audience, particularly playgoers at the extreme sides of the stage, and those in the Lords' rooms. Instead, Hermione stood beneath the 'fiery cloud' in the Heavens inside a circular curtain hanging from a hoop held up by attendants, at about the same spot where she had stood for trial inside a cage in 2.1. The actors stood around her, which meant less risk of playgoers seeing the 'statue' breathing. The varied responses to the staging of this seemed to demonstrate that naturalistic practices are not necessarily the most compelling. Michael Gould who played Polixenes felt that the scene is written in such a way that the audience does not need to see the statue; that the audience gets everything it needs from the words. 'I wish in retrospect we had been braver and not gone for the visual thing, that we had trusted the language, and put Hermione in the discovery space. There are so many lines dedicated to what was happening, and if the audience can see it anyway, it makes the lines seem redundant.' The emphasis the scene places on the description of the statue by the onlookers onstage was clearly a practical necessity to enable playgoers who could not see what was happening within the discovery space to *listen* and find out. Many of the lines found in the play which appear to be stating the obvious are often describing the invisible.

The central opening was used for the 'dead' Hermione to be laid there and later be transformed into the 'bear' that kills Antigonus at end of Act III, and it was used for the final *exeunt* of all those on stage apart from Autolycus.

The *Henry V* company tried out different ways of managing the curtains and decided that two stage hands would open each curtain by means of a pole so that the curtains were suspended like tent-flies for the English camp, and the same technique was used for the discovered tableau of the dead Boy. David Carnegie in an article on the use of stage-hangings at the original Globe very reasonably asks: 'in a theatre where stage attendants are constantly bringing in tables and banquets, carrying off dead bodies, and so forth, might it not be more likely that stage attendants opened and closed the traverse curtain when necessary in full view of the audience?'[5]

The central opening's hierarchical functioning was recognised in the *Henry V* staging, and given dramaturgical resonances when, for example, in contrast to the ceremonial drawing-back of the drapes of arras, the curtains were roughly pushed aside by the French nobles when they made their entrance. The central opening was mainly used for royal entrances, and for the final *exeunt*, and the flanking doors for other transitions. In the rehearsal room, a mock-up central opening and a balcony consisting of a wooden chair for the actor to stand on became the gates and walls of Harfleur, and a corner of the room where the props were stored became the French camp toward which Henry and his men looked nervously out as they sang the camp song that would have once rung out across a medieval battlefield.

Entrances and exits

Overlapping entrances and exits worked very well, and are usually a necessary piece of staging at the new Globe because it takes two or three lines for an actor to move from an entry door in the *frons* to the front of the stage.[6] If the stage is empty, the energy-levels in the theatre drop; and apart from the strictly practical point of having to solve the problem of how long it takes to move across such a deep stage, overlapping exists and entrances help to make a production seamless. They also, of course, help to speed up performance time.

Such overlapping can reduce running-time of the play by allowing a very short hiatus to mark the division of scenes.[7]

Beckerman's theory was that all players always enter through the same door and exit at the other. Others have argued that the player must always enter by the door he last exited through. Theories which have been put forward so far have tended to be just that – theoretical. Experience in playing the reconstructed Globe so far has suggested that inventiveness and expediency have been the determining factors in dictating the staging of any given entrance and exit. If the *frons scenae* is used for representing the walls, and the central opening the gates of Harfleur, you cannot use the central opening for the hierarchical entry of Henry, when he is supposed to be outside the city of Harfleur and demanding to be let in.

Allusions to the Natural Elements

Hamlet's 'brave o'erhanging firmament, this majestical roof fretted with golden fire' is the great canopy of the 'Heavens' which covers the stage. Its underside is painted with sun, moon, stars and clouds. It is to this that Lorenzo directs Jessica's gaze (and the audience's) when he says: 'Look how the floor of heaven/Is thick inlaid with patens of bright gold' in *The Merchant of Venice*. In *The Two Gentlemen of Verona* Sylvia stood on the balcony and pointed to the Moon painted on the 'Heavens' of the new Globe: 'Swear by the pale queen of night' ....

Several resonances were recovered from the texts when spoken under an open roof. In a Workshop led by director Sean Holmes, Hamlet was able to look up at the sky, point to a cloud, and declare that it was 'very like a whale', at which, most of us in the audience looked up to find out whether we agreed with him or not.

Performance-Time and the Weather

Performance-times are speeded up when it's raining. Actor Toby Cockerell pointed out that the actors could sense the playgoers wanting them to play faster. Mark Rylance found that it was like having to shout through a thunderstorm. It is not only rain falling that effects the acoustics so strongly. When the air is humid the actors have to speak their lines much louder; on a clear day they can judge the acoustics better and speak at their usual level. A surprisingly large number of groundlings stood it out in the rain. Audience responses – and actors' by-play with them – often lengthened performance-time by as much as fifteen minutes.

Performance-Time and Unscripted Moments

Performance-time is strongly affected by the actor–audience interaction, as one would expect. The new Globe is a natural environment for the practice of extemporization, as Hamlet snootily noted ('And let those that play your clowns speak no more than is set down for them; for there be of them that will themselves laugh to set on some quantity of barren spectators to laugh too…' 3.2.38–41) Audience applause, much more frequent than in conventional theatres, adds considerably to performance times.

Floor Covering – the Rushes

The rushes that were strewn across the stage for the duration of the performance for *Henry V* proved problematic at the beginning of the run. Quite a few of the actors felt the floor covering made movement too awkward, and there was much discussion among actors, designer, director, and stage management on whether to get rid of them. It was decided to keep experimenting with them – damping them down, making them shorter, spreading them more thinly, then more thickly, then more thinly again, and endless permutations of such (at one point, the director seemed always to be on stage at every available opportunity with a pair of shears snipping the rushes in two) In a fine example of the spirit of experimentation, which this theatre space seems to inspire, the actors persevered, clomping through the straw. Eventually, they found that the rushes helped rather than hindered the performance. They said it felt natural and helped them to create the sense of place. The question of the rushes proved to have a significance beyond that of its all-important stage-design one. This was an example of how performance at the new Globe will provide experiential evidence in the study of Shakespearean staging.

Historical Detail

To recover something of the knowledge about the play's events which the original Globe players and playgoers would have brought to a performance of the play, reference was frequently made to modern historians' studies of the battle of Agincourt and brought into discussions of how to play the military scenes. Particularly helpful was the information about the physical conditions of the actual French campaign. Holinshed's *Chronicles* was consulted in work on creating the sense of place in the Harfleur scenes. Rehearsing the passage where MacMorris and Jamy come from the mines to be met by Gower and Llewellyn became much less difficult once Holinshed had provided the important detail that the soldiers tunnelling under Harfleur's walls had been working underground for days without food or water. When the scene was transferred to the stage Jamy and McMorris would be rolling around the dirty building debris under the new Globe stage, blackening their faces with dust, and working up a heaving, exhausted breath before emerging through the trap along with bursts of smoke that were being deftly pumped out of the smoke-effect machine by stage manager, Jack Morrison, below.

Use of the Yard

Directors and actors in the first seasons were keen to use the yard as an extension of the playing-space. There is no clear evidence that the yard of the original Globe was used in this way. The yard at the new Globe was mostly used for entrances and exits through the groundlings. In some of the sessions in the Workshop season, the stage was not used at all and staging took place in the yard. In the Masque scene in *The Maid's Tragedy*, the acting space was extended into the yard: the King's throne was placed in the centre of the yard so that the masque enacted on stage was watched by the fictional character surrounded by the theatre audience.[8] In *Henry V* the yard was used for entrances and exits by Pistol, Llewellyn, Bardolph and Nym; and in *A Chaste Maid* the entrances of Whorehound's entourage and that of Sir Kix are made simultaneously through different auditorium doors, through the groundlings, and up on either side of the stage. The yard was used by characters before the play started when public notices forbidding the eating of meat during Lent were pinned up on the ground-level gallery posts. In *The Winter's Tale* 4.1, Time was played by Nicholas Le Prevost as a drunken vagrant barging his way through the groundlings in the yard, before managing to clamber up the five-foot height of the stage. After the interval in *The Two Gentlemen*, Thurio entered in a swimming costume and prepared to dive off the edge of the stage into the yard.

The Balcony

For the Opening season productions the balcony was used for seating playgoers, for dramatic action, and for musicians. Playgoers seated in the balcony or lords' rooms' completed the circle of ears which Webster described, and offered an opportunity for actors to experience the presence of an audience on all sides of the stage. For the playgoers, it presented a novel experience of being above the stage and the action, and the unexpected discovery that it was an excellent position for visibility and sightlines (except when the central opening is used as a discovery space). The traditional idea that these, the most expensive seats in the house, offered poor sightlines, and that the spectators sat in them primarily to be seen by the rest of the audience, has now to be re-examined. There has not been the opportunity to find out how staging the monument scene in *Antony and Cleopatra* works at the new Globe. Samuel Daniel's graphically detailed description of the use of the balcony in *The Death of Antony*, 1607 version, believed to be a description of the monument scene in Shakespeare's *Antony and Cleopatra*, is worth quoting at length for its suggestive implications for staging balcony scenes in productions at the new Globe.

> Which when his love
> His royal Cleopatra understood
> She sends with speed his body to remove,
> The body of her love imbru'd with blood.
> Which brought unto her tomb, (lest that the press
> Which came with him, might violate her vow)
> She draws him up in rolls of taffaty
> T'a window at the top, which did allow
> A little light unto her monument.

The bleeding Antony, being hoisted up the monument, showers blood on to the groundlings:

> There Charmian, and poor Iras, two weak maids
> Foretir'd with watching, and their mistress' care,
> *Tugg'd at the pulley, having n'other aids,*
> *And up they hoist the swounding body there*
> *Of pale Antonius, show'ring out his blood*
> *On th'under lookers, which their gazing stood.*

1 The stage and audience from the yard, *Henry V*: Williams (Rory Edwards), Gower (Vincent Brimble), Henry (Mark Rylance), Duke of Bedford (Nick Fletcher) and Llewellyn (David Fielder).

2 *The Maid's Tragedy*: the Wedding Masque. Proteus (Andrew Bridgmont), Boreas (Michael Gould), Sea Monsters (Dean Atkinson, Lucy Campbell, Polly Pritchett), Aeolus (Jonathan Bond), Night (Joy Richardson), Cynthia (Belinda Davison). Musicians (Toby Coles, Rachel Bunyan, Emily White, Pascal Wyse, Robin Hayward).

3 Detail of the 'Heavens' and the Lords' Room or Musicians' Room, *Henry V*: King of France (William Russell).

4 *Henry V*: musicians in the Musicians' Room: Michael Gregory, percussion; Keith McGowan, trumpet, curtal; Adrian Woodward, trumpet, cornett; Paul Sharp, trumpet, cornett; Abigal Newman, sackbut, trumpet.

5 The stage from the yard. *Henry V*: Exeter (Matthew
Scurfield), Ely (William Russell), Michael Gregory (musician), Canterbury
(John McEnery), Henry (Mark Rylance), Bedford (Nick Fletcher),
Westmorland (Bill Stewart), Scroop (Steven Skybell).

6 *Henry V*: Katherine (Toby
Cockerell), Isabel, Queen of
France (Christian Camargo),
Henry (Mark Rylance).

7 Period clothing for *Henry V*: Bedford (Matthew Scurfield).

8 Period clothing for *Henry V*: the central opening using fly tents for the English camp. Henry (Mark Rylance).

9 The stage showing the *frons scenae*, Lords' Room above the stage, marbelised columns, and the central opening flanked by two side doors. *Henry V*: Gloucester (David Lear), Henry (Mark Rylance); Bedford (Nick Fletcher), Exeter (Matthew Scurfield), Llewellyn (David Fielder).

10 *A Chaste Maid in Cheapside*: the duel between Whorehound (Rory Edwards) and Touchwood Junior (Christian Camargo).

11 *The Winter's Tale*: the sheep-shearing scene. Perdita (Anna-Livia Ryan) surrounded by 'sheep'.

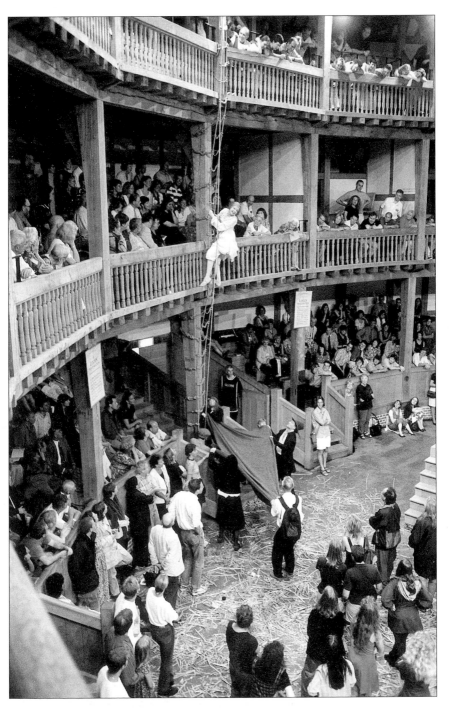

12 *A Chaste Maid in Cheapside*: using the yard for the chase. Moll (Katie MacNichol), Waterman (Nick Fletcher), Warden (Bill Stewart), Warden (Vincent Brimble), Attendant (Jack Morrison) and a Groundling.

13 Welcome Msomi's *Umabatha*, the 'Zulu Macbeth'; the procession of warriors.

And when they had now wrought him up half way
(Their feeble powers unable more to do)
The frame stood still, the body at a stay,
When Cleopatra all her strength thereto
Puts, with what vigour love, and care could use,
So that it moves again, and then again
It comes to stay. When she afresh renews
Her hold, and with reinforced power doth strain,
And all the weight of her weak body lays,
Whose surcharg'd heart more then her body weighs.
At length she wrought him up, and takes him in,
Lays his yet breathing body on her bed....
Samuel Daniel, The Death of Antony, 1607
(emphases added)

In the new Globe's *Henry V* production, the balcony and *frons scenae* were used as the walls of Harfleur, with the governor delivering his speech from the balcony, as would have been the case in the original staging. Witnesses of Hermione's trial in *The Winter's Tale* sat in the balcony to look down on the proceedings on-stage which suggested one way in which plays-within-plays (such as *Dream*'s 'Pyramus and Thisbe' and *Hamlet*'s 'The Mousetrap') might be staged at the new Globe. In *The Two Gentlemen of Verona*, the balcony was used by the outlaws to abseil on to the stage in Act 5; and the space beneath the balcony was used for covert effect in several scenes. Thurio sings his 'Who is Sylvia?' ballad there, accompanied by his hired musicians and with Proteus urging him on with his wooing, while Silvia is 'indoors' above. It is not surprising that one of the most brilliantly stage-managed scenes of Jacobean drama is the ingenious fusion of technical and dramaturgical meaning in Act II, Scene 2 of Middleton's *Women Beware Women*, possibly first performed at the Globe, in which a game of chess is being played on the main stage and a seduction scene is taking place at the same time in the balcony above.

The Trap Door

In *Henry V* the trap was used as the mouth of the tunnel under the walls of Harfleur from which MacMorris (Craig Pinder) and Jamy

(Nick Fletcher) emerged to be harangued by the scholar of war, Llewellyn (David Fielder), for not knowing their military engineering theory. The trap was also used as the cellar of the Eastcheap tavern in 2.1 from where Pistol (John McEnery) and Mistress Quickly (Vincent Brimble) could be heard noisily enjoying themselves before emerging in a state of *déshabillé* to join Bardolph and Nym. For the Masque in *The Maid's Tragedy*, the stage and *frons scenae* were covered in a huge midnight-blue drape, which was made to billow by performers who emerged from the covered stage-trap and slid through slits in the fabric to be revealed as Neptune, Boreas, some enormous strange sea-monsters, and trumpeters.

The Trap in the Heavens

Descents from the trap in the Heavens were experimented with in the Opening season. For the masque in *The Maid's Tragedy*, a traditional pulley was used to lower Cynthia (Belinda Davison), who remained suspended above the stage for the duration of the masque. For *A Chaste Maid*, ships' rigging was lowered from the trap for a spectacular chase in 4.2 down which the Waterman/Porter (Nick Fletcher) clambered. It enabled Moll (Katie MacNichol), the object of pursuit, to tumble down the rigging to be greeted by her waiting love, Touchwod Junior, with the words: 'What took you so long?' (Middleton's original line was 'What made you so long?') which brought the house down every time. Production manager Richard Howey, and head of stage, John Hale, in charge of the technicals for this production, explained that the pulley and technology that was used in the original theatre would have been very similar to what they had set up for the descents. The main difference between then and now is that it was necessary for stage managers to wear mikes to co-ordinate safety procedures.

The Stage Decoration[9]

Playgoers (and actors) tend to get a shock when they first come inside the reconstructed Globe and find a stage richly coloured in ornamentation. The elaborate iconography and the brightly painted decoration, suggesting the Elizabethan emblematic conception of the stage as a microcosm of the real world, are richly allusive. The Muse of Tragedy and of Comedy on the second level of the *frons scenae* proclaims the theatre's ability to present all things under the heavens. A celestial scene resembling a night sky, with forms of the zodiac encircling a supernal light, are painted on 'The heavens', the canopy which covers the stage, and the dramatic muses.

FURNITURE

The first productions showed that 'place-setting' and 'mood-creating' stage furniture is rarely a good idea in an open-air playhouse. Sit on chairs, on stools or on the platform itself for anything other than brief moments, and the energy goes. Kings sitting in their chairs of state, as one would expect, can get away with using this stage furniture, perhaps because they are the focal and aural point of any scene they are in, and because the chair of state, being large and impressive, does not get swallowed up in the vast space of the stage platform. A Victorian-style Windsor wing chair used in *The Two Gentlemen*, for example, looked incongruous on the Globe stage, as if it had strayed in from a West End Chekhov production. But it also presented a practical obstacle. The wings blocked audience sightlines and audibility from one side of the stage. The bringing on of props such as a table laid with glasses and plates and food presents practical questions that can affect dramaturgical aspects of performance. If a character is delivering a soliloquy at the end of a scene where such furniture and props have been used, when do you take them off? After the character exits? When the stage is empty of figures it goes dead, and this would slow down performance time. If the props are taken off stage during the soliloquy, it presents a distraction, and means that the character would not be alone with the audience. *The Winter's Tale* staging made bold and elaborate use of large items of furniture and props, with the stage filled up with huge tractor tyres for thrones.

MUSIC

The reconstructed Globe has encouraged a renewed interest in the function of music in the staging of plays in the early modern amphitheatres. As we have seen, with no stage design – sets, controlled lighting, and elaborate properties – music becomes much more important in the creation of mood and meaning. It becomes an expressive form in its own right, and research into and use of the musical forms, arrangements and instruments of Shakespeare's time has brought another dimension to the preparation of the plays for the space. Composer Claire van Kampen, music director on *The Two Gentlemen of Verona, The Winter's Tale,* and *A Chaste Maid in Cheapside,* says: 'To make up for the absence of lights and other theatrical devices, the music has to be very specific to what is going on on stage. You have to put the sounds together very carefully, minimally, so that the economy of sound draws the audience into the story.' At the time of writing, Van Kampen is researching music possibilities for *The Merchant of Venice,* particularly the Italian madrigals that were imported to England in Shakespeare's time. It is a play that is suffused with music and it will be interesting to experience the play with the importance of music so strongly emphasized in an open playhouse – when authentic music on original instruments is played 'above' in the music-room which Lorenzo hears 'on such a night' and utters his paean to the power of music (5.1). It has been clear that when music was used it was an integral part of the whole performance, and as a way of making meaning on the stage that could be comparable to that of words and action. It takes on a much larger role in creating and shaping mood and a sense of place than in usual modern productions and, as the first seasons have shown, can offer a more expressive means of doing so than a designed set or controlled lighting.

COSTUMES

Henry V and *A Chaste Maid in Cheapside* were the first productions to try out the rich colours of authentic dress against the colourful decor of the *frons scenae.* For *Henry V* Jenny Tiramani, the Globe's 'tirewoman' or wardrobe-keeper, re-created sixteenth-century clothing, using original fabrics and, where possible, organic dyes like madder, weld, indigo, safranin and carmine, and the clothing was handstitched and much of it handwoven. Actors' responses were almost uniformly positive: the most frequent comment being that it was much easier to wear authentically made clothes rather than theatrical costumes.

Re-created clothing of the period which allows for freedom of movement and the all-important body-language required by the new Globe space has shown that what an actor wears, and how he or she wears it can have specific dramaturgical consequences, in terms of characterization, blocking and social hierarchy and etiquette. In *A Chaste Maid*, the elaborate and extended attention to the social significances of Allwit's putting on and off of his hat makes dramaturgical sense (and, of course, enriches the irony) when the habitually hatted character of Allwit (Mark Rylance) suddenly doffs his headgear in the presence of his wife's lover, the physically and morally atrophied Sir Walter Whorehound (Rory Edwards). Clothing for *A Chaste Maid* consisted of inventive and bizarre examples of Jacobean apparel. Whorehound sported a two-foot high 'spike' of hair that grew from the top of his head and seemed to be futilely pointing towards the heavens while his white pallor spoke of the physical surfeit and spiritual atrophy of a diseased body and soul. The chaste maid's mother, Maudlin (Amelda Brown) had bright-orange hair that made her look as though she were permanently fixed to an electric current, and a 90-degrees farthingale which circled her waist like a giant saucer, and her husband, Yellowhammer, the goldsmith (Matthew Scurfield), in leather apron and bottle-lens spectacles, was permanently covered in dust, the filthy lucre of his trade – a shining example of glittering capitalism.

For *The Winter's Tale*, costumes were in keeping with the overall design of the production which was inspired by African and Asian cultures. The Sicilian characters were dressed in brown, the Bohemians in blue; all were barefoot, and the actors' hair was styled with mud. In keeping with the giant tyres used as thrones and shrines, the jewellery was made from recycled bolts, screws and chains, worn round arms, ankles and necks. Perdita's costume was a green dress with woven flowers, and she also wore an intricate head-dress festooned with flowers. The costumes were comfortable clothes designed for the greatest possible freedom for the body language that was emphasised in the production. For Francis Beaumont and John Fletcher's *The Maid's Tragedy*, costumes were kept monochromatic and fairly non-defined for the main action. In the masque, Cynthia (Belinda Davison) wore a cream Jacobean costume with high-fanned collar as she was suspended in the air above the 'sea monsters', who emerged through slits in a huge blue skirt of waves covering the stage.

The Two Gentlemen of Verona was performed in modern designer clothes (except for Launce who wore a tweed jacket, cloth cap and flannels) which led to some oddly disparate dress where the characters seemed to belong to different plays.

VOICE

It is tempting to claim that tone of voice 'is everything' in the Globe. How we hear a character becomes a more important element in our experience of the play. 'Aural story-telling', Mark Rylance, says, is 'the medium for everything' at the reconstructed Globe. Many modern productions of *Richard III* have achieved powerful effects in staging the sudden change in Richard's character in the second half of the play, from the perversely compelling erotic monster who seduces us into guilty complicity of his murderous route to the throne, and the distant figure of the newly crowned King on a chair of state that seems to have robbed him of both his power and his relationship with the audience. No longer sharing confidences with us in the low tones that are possible on the perimeters of the stage platform, Richard literally moves away from us to ascend the throne on its dais several feet in front of the *frons* and address his words to the court-audience on stage. This contrast, I suspect, will be more pronounced when the play is produced in the space at the new Globe where the actor's position on the stage can itself make meaning, and where, by means of the actor's modulation of tone, the voice that had coaxed us into an unwilling submission to his charm is gone, and he no longer talks to us. The play's remarkable experimentation with the contrasting effects of different kinds of rhetorical language – particularly that between Margaret's formal speech and the women's ritualized chanting, and Richard of Gloucester's stylistically nimble, playful self-dramatizing rhetoric will receive a literal new resonance and dramaturgical meaning.

J. L. Styan has told us perhaps all we really need to know about Shakespeare's use of sound and action when he said that 'What is heard directs, and yet seems to echo, what is seen.' In an open public amphitheatre, this unusual synthesis of sound and sight becomes manifest. Michael Gould, who played Polixenes and Diphilus, said: 'We developed quite big boomy voices thinking that was what we would need in the space, but when we moved into the space we realized just how intimate it could be.... I found that if there was clarity of intention in a very quite moment, I could hear the words because I really wanted to hear them.' Motivated movement, motivated speech, emoting on the line, not between lines, can prompt the audience to a kind of motivated listening, as it were.

J. L. Styan has described how Shakespeare modulated the reciprocal process of sight and hearing, the aural shaping of the plays in performance.

> Speech rather than invented business, the rise and fall of tone in a scene, the pace of playing, with its variations, and the total sound pattern of the play should have an unshakeable place in the creative experience.... An idea in a play may echo and reverberate. When it is sounded again in another tone or on another tongue, the resulting ironies point to the values underlying the drama.[10]

Jeanette Nelson, Voice Coach on the four productions of the Opening season, said: 'The acoustics are very resonant. The theatre flatters the actor's voice. The actors hear their voice coming back at them. It works better when full than when there's no audience. Acoustically, it likes people.' Andrew Wade in his Voice workshop felt that it is not a question of volume, but of pitch, and of finding ways to use what he calls 'the muscularity' of Shakespeare's language. Philip Stafford talked of Shakespeare's language being so powerful that 'it hurls you bodily on to your opponent'. Theatre director, Richard Cottrell, who began his workshop thinking the actors would need to speak very loudly, ended it by saying: 'Maybe it's not about speaking loudly. Natural speaking is better than roaring.' And one confirmation of this was when one actor sitting in the middle gallery told his fellow-actor who was speaking on stage: 'You're shouting.'

Many actors thought it was difficult to judge voice and audibility and found themselves shouting at first, when they discovered that what was needed was greater projection, definition and clarity, not volume. Belinda Davison, who played Hermione in *The Winter's Tale* and Cynthia in *The Maid's Tragedy*, said that voice-work was particularly important: on stage for the first time, she found, as the other actors did, that 'it was easy to strain the voice, because the demands on the diaphragm are great'. As the actors became used to the space and gained more vocal confidence, they did not have to push the sound so much, it was easier on the diaphragm. David Fielder, who played Llewellyn in *Henry V* and Davy in *A Chaste Maid*, found that you can 'pull the sound in quite small'; that 'you don't have to shout – it can be very gentle'. Polly Pritchett who played Emilia in *The Winter's Tale* and Olympias in *The Maid's Tragedy* felt that the greatest challenge is vocal. 'There is no set, everything has to be in your voice. The old-fashioned voice-training that a lot of us have thrown away, that we felt we didn't need, because we spend so much time working on television and in much smaller theatres, where you've got the image to help you, comes back in this theatre. You have to be able to use your voice to describe everything.' William Russell (French King, Tutor) said: 'I have a feeling that the Globe theatre could take more musicality in the actual speaking of the verse – which is difficult for modern actors to do. I don't ask for a return to great sonorous voice work, but a sense of the music and the rhythms and the poetry, can be employed and explored with more daring and courage.'

Part II
Staging History:
Henry V in Preparation and Performance

5

Preparing the Play
for the Globe Space

THE TEXT

Before the start of rehearsals, director Richard Olivier and Globe artistic director Mark Rylance went through the New Cambridge edition (ed. Andrew Gurr) to cut about 20 per cent of the play.[1] The aim was to make cuts of roughly equal length from each act/scene/ Chorus as a means of reducing performance time – in keeping with the production's 'authentic brief' (see 'Research' section below). Reference was made to the First Folio in the decision-making process. Research fellow Pauline Kiernan was consulted about the cuts made in Act 5. It was decided to leave the Epilogue completely intact, and not to cut 20 per cent as planned after discussions about its significances for the overall meaning of the play.

At this stage of preparing the play for performance, the cut text was given to the actors with the understanding that it was a 'provisional' script. The scripts were A4 enlarged photocopies of the pages of the Cambridge edition with the cut lines still readable beneath the deletion scores.

Once rehearsals began, the cuts would be discussed among the company at various stages from readthrough to improvised character work, first run, and so on.

Cuts That Were Reinstated
1.2.53; 3.3.6–7; 3.3.57 ('Marry, I wad full fain hear some questions 'tween you two'); 3.4.39–41; 3.7.46–7; 3.7.110–14.
4.1.55–6; 4.1.195–6; 4.3.53–4; 4.7.96–104; 4.8.79–83; 5.2.215–23; 5.2.274–83; 5.2.291–3; 5.2.299–310.

Additional Cuts
4.1.69 ('I warrant you, you'); 70–2; 5.2.209 ('My comfort is that old age, that ill layer-up of'); 210–11; 212 ('wear me, better and better').

93

Doubling, Cuts and Changes

When the play was cut it was decided to split the Chorus between six of the characters in the play. Richard Olivier explains: 'Within the play we wanted to set up the idea that it was a company of actors telling a story. We couldn't afford an actor to play just the Chorus, and we thought about using one character from the play, but quickly decided that it would draw too much attention to that one character, when we're trying to draw attention more to the story. I thought it was better to draw attention to a certain character in each act – a character who has a certain impact in each act. It developed from there, really. Of course, the Prologue should have been given by Sam (Wanamaker), but failing Sam's physical presence it seemed to us that the Artistic Director should do it, although Mark was very much against doing it at first.'

Prologue Chorus played by 'Henry V'
Act II Chorus played by 'Duke of Exeter'
Act III Chorus played by 'Llewellyn'
Act IV Chorus played by 'Michael Williams'
Act V Chorus played by 'Pistol'
Epilogue Chorus played by 'French King'

Major Doubling/Trebling

The *Henry* company consisted of 15 actors to play 44 to 45 parts. This required heavy doubling. Academic adviser Andrew Gurr provided notes on doubling, from a base cast of 15, the number counted by Platter for a performance of *Julius Caesar*, almost certainly at the Globe, in 1599.[2]

Katherine/Boy
Pistol/Archbishop of Canterbury/Governor of Harfleur
French King/Bishop of Ely/Erpingham
Isabel, the French Queen/Louis, the Dauphin/Thomas Grey
Michael Williams/Duke of Orleans/Duke of Burgundy
Constable of France/John Bates/Scroop
Lord Rambures/MacMorris/Earl of Cambridge/Alexander Court
Llewellyn/Le Fer
Bardolph/Montjoy/Alice
Gower/Mistress Quickly
Jamy/Duke of Bedford
Earl of Westmorland/Nym/English Herald

RESEARCH WORK ON THE PLAY

Following Sam Wanamaker's wish that at least one production of every season would be as 'authentic' as possible, it was decided that one production, *Henry V*, would be given an 'authentic brief' in the Opening season. Olivier says: 'The way I took it was that we would, as a production, undertake to explore certain authentic production methods or styles. Not that we were trying to make the whole thing as it would have been in the sixteenth century.'

The 'Authentic Brief'
'Authentic' production methods used for *Henry V* involved:

- An all-male cast. A 'boy-actor' played Katherine. Young male actors played Alice and the French Queen. A male actor played Mistress Quickly.
- Cuts to the text to speed up performance time.
- Five interval-free performances (with two-minute pauses between each acts necessary for costume-changes).
- Doubling of parts.
- Extensive historical costume research and practice by Jenny Tiramani. The *Henry V* costume team hand-stitched and dyed all clothing with original materials using dress-making methods of the period, with original fastenings, including undergarments that would not necessarily be seen.
- Authentic weapons: swords and crossbows.
- Historical music research by the Globe's Director of Early Music, Phillip Pickett, including the use of period instruments: sackbut, cornett, natural trumpet, slide-trumpet, curtal, drum. The music director and the musicians held extensive rehearsals throughout the preparation period. The flourishes, alarums, tuckets, parleys and retreats – the trumpet calls commanding the horse soldiers and drum rhythms commanding the foot soldiers – were authentic for the English and the French, including the different pitch which the French used, which was lower than the English calls. Philip Pickett explains: 'All the trumpet tunes are the originals that would have been played at the time. In the days when standing armies did not exist and alliances changed rapidly, it was necessary for the various commands to be standardized throughout Europe. The original audience would have recognized the different meanings of the calls': the sound for a retreat,

for example, and the alarum Henry hears in 4.7 which has the specific meaning that tells him, 'The French have reinforced their scattered men', and prompts him to order every soldier to kill his prisoners. A discussion about these included the point that although modern audiences would not know the difference between a flourish, a parley, an alarum and a retreat, the company agreed that by being aware of the distinction, the actions and responses of the soldiers to what they hear during the 'battle' was a positive help in playing the scene, and that this would, in turn, instill belief on the part of the audience. The timing of the flourishes and parleys was given a great deal of rehearsal time.

The incidental music consisted of arrangements by Philip Pickett of original material with a warlike background and included 'The March of Foot' from a keyboard piece by William Byrd, 'The Battle'; arrangements of material from Andrew Newman's 'Pavan', and from four pieces from the 'Mulliner Book': 'La Bounette'.

The fourteenth-century camp-song of the English army, 'The Souldiers', was sung in English camps up to 1800.

All gallant knights
Don for the day's fight
The breast plates so bright
To battle their foes.
The valiant steed prances
And with spirit dances.
Daylight advances
The night is near gone. [The hour is near come]

The company was offered two alternatives for the final lines of each stanza: 'The night is near gone', or 'The hour is near come'. The actors felt that the reference to the night in the first was more suitable and in keeping with the mood of night and the coming of the dawn they were trying to create. The discussion led on to one of several relating to the creation of mood and location on the Globe stage. It was agreed that anything that might help the actors and audience to imaginatively create the sense of the passing of the night, not only in this instance (on the eve of the battle of Agincourt in *Henry V*), but in any play which had night-scenes, would enhance the performance. Throughout the rehearsal period, the director and actors were conscious that they would be playing in daylight and usually with the sun shining down through the open roof of the theatre, and that there would not be stage lighting-effects.

The camp song of the French army in the production is also fourteenth-century:

> Celle qui m'a demandé
> Argent pour être m'amie
> Elle m'a fait grand vilénie
> Jamais je ne l'aimerai,
> Bon gré en ai sainté Gemme
> Lui en fault il de retour.
> Ne lui doibt il pas sufire
> Si se lui donne amour.
> Je la quite en bonné joy
> Et feray une aultré amie
> Puis qu'el demandé partie
> D'argent qu'avou elle et moy.
> Celle qui m'a demandé
> Argent pour etre m'amye
> Elle me fait grand villénie
> J'amais je ne l'aimerai.

At the end of Act 4, two of the actors were to sing *Non nobis* and *Te Deum*, which are specified in the text:

King: Do we all holy rites.
  Let there be sung *Non nobis* and *Te Deum*

4.8.114–15.

This was sung in the Lords' rooms to signal the end of the act.

- Research fellow Pauline Kiernan provided video film of a special performance of authentic jigs which had been researched and directed by academic Antony Green at the Theatre Department of Bretton Hall Institute, which Kiernan and Mark Rylance had attended in the spring of 1997. The Globe company did experimental work on authentic jigs,[3] particularly the songs, with Philip Pickett, such as 'A proper new ballad, entitled 'Rowland's

Godson' to the tune of 'Loth to Depart'.[3] Work was then done on producing an 'authentic' jig in present-day language to come after each performance of *Henry V*. The company were reluctant to abandon what they felt were the positive benefits to both actors and audience of performing a jig at the end of a show, namely the sense of 'completing' an experience which had been shared by actors and audience. After much discussion, and further work on the new words for a jig, it was decided that the preparation involved was in danger of using up valuable time and energy which the company felt was needed for *Henry V*. It was decided to find an alternative to an authentic jig.

As the actors' preparation of the play had involved playing African drums, which had led to the idea of opening each performance of the play with the actors coming on stage beating the floor with their staves, it was decided to end each performance with all the actors coming back on stage and drumming. The actors felt that this had grown naturally from the work they had done on preparing the play for performance, and that it would be, in a sense, this particular production's 1997 version of an 'Elizabethan jig'.

- Management of the stage was planned to be as close to Elizabethan conditions as was possible within the safety constraints of the modern Globe. At the first production meeting of the play, in which technical requirements for the production were discussed, Mark Rylance said that the aim was 'to try not to use modern technology unless we really have to'. Stage management were not in period clothing and it was necessary, for safety reasons, to wear headphones.
- Use of stage trap.
- Use of the lords' rooms/music room in the balcony above the stage by seated playgoers.
- Use of the music room by musicians (although there is no evidence for this at the original Globe until 1609).
- Use of a cannon in the gable (from a replica of *The Golden Hinde*)
- Ticket prices set at rough equivalents of Elizabethan playhouse prices (as with all productions at the Globe)

Deliberately non-authentic aspects of the production included extensive actor-use of the yard as a means of access to the stage, for which there is no evidence. Stepping devices were placed against the stage for actors to climb up on to the stage from the yard, and to exit from the stage. The playing of African drums was a deliberate anachronism intended to represent the 'heartbeat' of the Globe space – an organic building that breathes along with both playgoers and actors during performance.

Pauline Kiernan provided guidelines and research materials for various aspects of the 'authentic brief'. Designer Jenny Tiramani researched costume and design authenticity (including the uses of rushes on the stage). Andrew Gurr provided the director with suggestions concerning the original staging of the play. The aim, says Olivier, was to decide what elements were going to be 'authentic' and 'hopefully to reinvigorate those authentic methods'.

In the rehearsal room, a 'research table' was set up which the company was encouraged to make use of. This included a facsimile of the First Folio (which was regularly consulted), books on medieval military campaigns, particularly Christopher Hibbert's *Agincourt*, academic studies of the play, source material such as Holinshed, and so on. Specialists in Elizabethan costume, manners and sword-bearing visited the rehearsal-room several times to demonstrate movement in costume, hair styles, and social etiquette. The research fellow attending rehearsals (Pauline Kiernan) was included in discussions of the play, offered material about the play and its sources, and advised on textual cruxes, characterization, and Elizabethan theatrical conditions, and provided information requested by the director and actors.

The preparation also included the reading and discussion of myths and fairy tales, particularly the story of St George and the Dragon, as well as literary texts, such as the medieval *Romance of the Rose* translated by Chaucer, and its images of the maiden as a walled garden. Peter Dawkins provided major contributions on western philosophical ideas of the Elizabethan period. Early on in the rehearsal period the whole company spent a weekend at a disused army camp in the country to work on the play and to have the opportunity of exploring the 'brotherhood' theme of the play. This involved ritual work on learning to look on death, of finding ways to gain a deeper understanding of the experiences of the battlefield, dealing with death and survival. The weekend was intended to give the cast an opportunity to improvise scenes with more freedom and time than is usually afforded in the rehearsal-room.

IN THE REHEARSAL ROOM

7 April–17 May

- *7 April*: First readthrough, with approximately 20 per cent cuts, without intervals, without jig. This lasted two hours and 50 minutes.
- Mark-ups with accurate measurements of the stage and mock-pillars in their correct positions. Director Richard Olivier talked to the company about the importance of getting used to the dimensions of the stage and the positions of the pillars.
- A mock-up 'central opening' (coat-stands and white sheets) and hangings.
- A mock-up 'balcony' for the Harfleur scenes – a wooden chair for the actor to stand on became the 'gates' and the rehearsal room wall became the 'walls' of Harfleur.
- Items of furniture were tried out in the rehearsal room and most were rejected before the company took the play on to the stage. As Olivier explains: 'Before we started rehearsals I think we were planning on four stools, two different-sized tables, two daises, two thrones, a sail for the Southampton dock, and various other bits and pieces, and gradually as we went through rehearsing we just found the design naturally eroding. Almost every time we'd done a scene with furniture, we'd say. "Right, let's try and do it without the props", and every time we did it without, the scene was better.' Olivier says, 'I felt that as long as there was a kind of truth to the story-telling then the building would support that. For me, the ideas such as the one we tried out for the traitor scene, playing it as an official ceremony with seven stools placed in a formal arrangement, were getting in the way of the narrative. We didn't want clutter. We didn't want things getting in the way of the story.'
- Props were kept to a minimum.
  Props List

Act/Scene	Description	Character
1.1	Genealogical books	Canterbury, Ely
1.2	Throne on dais	
1.2	A 'tun' of tennis balls	Ambassador
2.1	'Papers of arrest'	Cambridge, Scroop, Grey
2.4	Scroll	Exeter
3.1	Scaling ladders	

Contd.

3.7	Drum and colours, English	King
	Coin for Montjoy	
4.6	Hand-ties	Prisoners
4.8	Money: crowns and shilling	Llewellyn, Attendants
	Papers, French and English Dead	Exeter (later Herald)
5.1	Leek	Llewellyn
	Cudgel	Llewellyn

- Movement and Voice Work: classes attended by actors every rehearsal morning to help physical stamina to keep body and voice supple, but also with the specific purpose of preparing for the particular physical configuration of stage and audience in the Globe space and its acoustics.
- Walking in a wide circle around the 'stage' looking at different 'playgoers' as individuals.
- Many of the blocking changes within the rehearsal room were prompted by the consideration of the Globe stage and its audience. For example, early on in rehearsals of 4.1. when Williams, Bates and Court are discussing the justice of war, the scene was tried with them all sitting down. Interestingly, even in the rehearsal room such blocking made the scene flat, and was rejected. Instead, long diagonal blocking was tried and, again interestingly, felt to be better suited to the intimacy of the scene.
- Blocking and timing were constantly being worked out for the intervals and Chorus at each act. Chorus' exits and characters' entrances overlapped.
- Actors rehearsed scenes blindfold for night scenes.
- Actors rehearsed imagining the Globe audience as the English army and the auditorium as the Agincourt battlefield. The first time the Act V Chorus was run in character, the research fellow made the point that at the line 'You may imagine him at Blackheath . . .', the play's original audiences would have been aware that Blackheath was just downstream from the Globe, the playwright's cue, perhaps, for the audience to look over their shoulders as if waiting to see Henry V in his 'bruised helmet' and his 'bended sword' – something which the 1997 Globe audience might also do.

- Tried out having a French prisoner killed on stage – and rejected it.
- Pauline Kiernan asked if the company could try reinstating the cuts from the 'French dead' speech in 4.8, making the point that the individual naming of the dead, the emphasis on the importance of the social/political status of the majority of them, and the total number lost had the powerful effect of reinforcing the reality of the number of French losses, and gave a balance to the sense of waste on both sides. The speech was tried out with all the names being spoken. After a discussion, the director said 'we won't make a decision yet'. The reinstating of the cuts was tried every time the speech was rehearsed. It was decided to reinstate five lines:

> So that in these ten thousands they have lost
> There are but sixteen hundred mercenaries.
> The rest are princes, barons, lords, knights, squires,
> And gentlemen of blood and quality.

(79–83)

- In the second half of the rehearsal period, rushes were strewn on the floor for the actors to get used to moving on them. The actors playing women practised gliding across the rushes in crinoline petticoats and practice wigs.
- The handmade leather shoes and boots were also introduced into rehearsals early on.
- Costume, which has been re-termed 'clothing' to describe authentic dress in Globe productions, was introduced as early as possible. The hand-sewn undershirts were provided by the costume department as soon as it was possible in the rehearsal period so that actors could start to feel in the earliest stages of working on the play what it would be like wearing them. Female characters more practice skirts and practice wigs for the same reason.
- Real swords, shields and helmets, provided by Renaissance sword-fights expert Philip Stafford, were used to get used to moving about with unfamiliar, heavy weights.
- Throughout the preparation period the company concentrated a great deal on ritual work, which was reflected in the director's emphasis on experiencing work on the play as a journey of

discovery as a 'circle' of 'storytellers', which is how the company was encouraged to see their role for when they took the play on to the stage and performed it for the Globe audience in the Wooden 'O'. The rituals they performed included those on learning to look at death. The director placed particular importance on findings ways for the actors to have an understanding of the horrors of war and of what it must be like to go into battle with your unit. The company would improvise scenes, not based on physical battle, but on focusing on the moments before the battle, then on coming out alive and finding everyone else dead.

- The military history of Henry V's French campaign was researched and discussed. Christopher Hibbert's *Agincourt* was regularly consulted by everyone, and provided valuable information on the gruelling hardships and extreme length of the campaign.

- *17 May*: Run the play for first time. No interval. Three hours. Director's notes on the first run:
- Costumes and space will change volume levels and sight lines.
- You need to fill the space out to the sides.
- Motivate moves.
- We need to brush up on etiquette.
- 2.1: Sword fighting is messy and needs sorting out.
- 3.7: Avoid a three-man line-up. Mud in the bog. You need to all agree on the extent you're getting stuck, not one person looking knee-deep and another ankle-deep.
- The French are fencing with words. The scene is character-led, not information-led.
- 4.1 and 4.2: Exits messy and need working out. It will be easier in the theatre.
- 4.6: Prisoners. Screaming heard from off-stage death scenes: we'll see how this all works when we get on to the stage.
- A lot of the blocking and sightlines will need to be worked on when we get the play on to the stage. We need to be flexible.

6

Taking the Play
on to the Stage

Rehearsals on Stage: 20–27 May

On 20 May 1997 the play was taken on to the Globe stage for the first time; this was the first day of technical rehearsals of the play.

- Long rushes were strewn on the stage and damped down.
- A builders' scaffolding tower was still being used at the sides of the stage, and the huge crane was still in use in the yard.
- The mechanism of the stage trap was still being worked out by master craftsman Peter McCurdy, architect Jon Greenfield, production manager Richard Howey, stage manager, Jack Morrison, and head of stage, John Cole during the first stage rehearsals.
- For 1.3. Bardolph comes up from the trap, followed by Nym. The two hear saucy noises from under the trap: Mistress Quickly, smoothing her dishevelled clothes, and Pistol, adjusting his trousers, emerge from the trap.

  Nym and Pistol stand on either side of the open trap in their repeatedly deferred sword-fight.
- Audibility and visibility were tested in all parts of the auditorium on the first day the company took the play on to the stage. Actors took turns to take up positions in all three galleries, particularly at the 'sides' of the stage and in the yard to test the sound. The actors on stage tried facing the *frons scenae* to test the audibility of consonants and syllables. John McEnery tried out the acoustics with his Act 5 Chorus lines and exclaimed that 'It all comes back at you'. One problem that had been anticipated from the experience of the Prologue season was actors' difficulty in hearing their cues when waiting behind the *frons scenae*. Holes were drilled in the two side entrance-doors, and tested out.
- Musicians tested out the Lords' Rooms above the stage.
- Designer Jenny Tiramani and her team of costume-makers worked round the clock to enable full costume to be worn by

the characters. Actors practised getting used to wearing authentic, thin-soled leather shoes.

- There was a voice class taken by the company voice coach Jeanette Nelson on day one. Audibility was tested by Jeanette Nelson, Richard Olivier and Pauline Kiernan from different parts of the auditorium. Jeanette Nelson thought that the theatre 'flatters the actor's voice'. She commented, 'the actors hear their voice coming back at them.' Nelson felt the actors would be needing 'a lot of warming up of the voice before performances'. Jeanette Nelson's notes were to do with clarity more than with volume.
- Sightlines were tested from every part of the theatre by the director and research fellow. Richard Olivier emphasised to the actors the importance of playing to the sides and to all levels of the auditorium.

The chair of state for 1.2. was a throne on a dais and canopy placed a few feet in front of the central opening. Richard Olivier urged the actors to 'Be aware of the pillars. Be aware of the people watching behind you!' When the French messenger stands in front of one of the pillars to deliver his speech, he is given a note by the director to stand in a position more visible to playgoers at that side of the stage.

BLOCKING

The director and actors were already prepared to find that the blocking which had been tried out in the rehearsal room would need to be changed/slightly altered/refined. The first blocking to be worked out was the opening, when the cast come on stage through the central opening and take up positions for the drumming introduction to the play. It was choreographed to make maximum use of the *three* large dimensions of the stage: the actors stood in positions in all key points of the stage so that the company would embrace every part of the auditorium. Richard Olivier reminded the actors of the presence of playgoers at the 'sides' of the stage on all three levels. Pauline Kiernan tested out sightlines from these positions, taking into account the obstructions of the scaffolding, which everyone was hoping would be taken down before the first public performance. After Henry delivered the Prologue, the cast formed a phalanx, and retreated from the stage through the central opening with their backs to the *frons*. The company quickly began to adapt to the blocking demands of the Globe stage on this first day. Several actors felt that it was a natural environment to play in – that an actor was able to feel connected to another even with some distance between them. This is an important point about the Globe space: that it encourages blocking in long diagonals.

The *Henry V* actors rapidly discovered that you need to *move* on this stage. John McEnery (Canterbury) and William Russell (Ely) in the first scene of the play found that by coming on to the stage from a side entrance and walking straight alongside the edge of the side of the stage, around the outside of the pillar and along the edge of the front of the stage on to the second pillar, they could conduct their conversation and move at the same time in such a way as to allow all parts of the audience to see them.

For the Harfleur scene (3.4), Bardolph, Pistol, Nym and the Boy run through the yard, carrying a ladder, which they lean up against the stage at one side, and climb up on to the stage. In this production the ladder was not used, as it would have been in original performances, for the English soldiers to scale the wall to climb up on to the balcony. Llewellyn comes through the yard and steps up on beer-barrels placed up against a corner of the stage. King Henry and his men enter through one of the two side entry doors on the stage because the balcony above the central opening is to represent the wall; and the central opening will become the gates of Harfleur when the Governor invites the English to 'Enter our gates': Henry and his men 'enter the Town' through the gates. As soon as this moment is played on the Globe stage, we believe that Henry is facing the town of Harfleur. As he turns to face the *frons* and says 'the town', it is Harfleur. The creation of 'place' by the simple act of 'looking' at whatever that place is supposed to be, is a marked characteristic of this space. The stage trap 'becomes' the entrance to the tunnel which MacMorris and Jamy have dug under the walls of Harfleur.

21 May: Second Day of Technical Rehearsals on Stage

The timing for cannon-fire and smoke from the trap at end of 3.1 was rehearsed. The cannon is fired from over the stage in the gable, after Henry's final line: 'Cry "God for Harry, England and St George!"' and, simultaneously, smoke rises from the trap. This was tried out four times.

Much work was done on blocking/movement with the pillars. Different arrangements of entrances were tried out for scenes with many characters on the stage. Several entrances worked better when a character entered by a side entrance, and walked in an L-shape around the outside of the stage pillar. In 3.2 diagonal movement inside the pillars was replaced by movement outside the pillars for Llewellyn and for Jamy.

Several blocking arrangements were found to work particularly well for playgoers in the top gallery at the side of the stage, next to the *frons*. For example, in 2.4. the chair of state and canopy is brought on by stage-hands through the central opening, followed by members of the French court. The French King sits, the courtiers spread out. Exeter enters stage right, walks in an L-shape along the side edge of the stage and around the outside of the stage-right pillar, to deliver his lines to the King in front of the stage pillar. The Dauphin stands to the King's immediate right, crosses the stage in a diagonal to the stage-left pillar and speaks in front of it. The working-out of the blocking for this scene was a particularly helpful example of how to make multiple-character scenes work on the Globe stage for all sections of the audience – what might be called '3-D acting'.

A great deal of attention was paid to the music. Trumpets were tested out on the balcony, then behind the *frons*. Musicians came on stage at different points to play alarums and flourishes.

There were three try-outs of the English camp song: first sung by English 'soldiers' behind the musicians in the balcony; then in the central opening, then hidden from the audience behind the *frons*.

For the beginning of 4.1. the English army came on stage slowly with spread-out blocking. They looked out across the tops of the heads of the groundlings to the 'French camp'. The creation of 'place' was instantaneous. The actors playing the English were focusing more and more on the French camp 'over there'; that is, across the yard. Time was spent experimenting with the best place to have the French camp-song sung. In the space behind the music-room in the balcony? Or (as was decided) outside one of the entrances to the yard, so that the English were looking towards the source of the sound of the French singing above the heads of the groundlings in the yard? The English army *exeunt*, leaving Williams, Bates and Court on stage.

Blocking for 4.1 came next. It is interesting that this pivotal scene, much worked on in the rehearsal room until it had become a scene that 'catches fire', played rather flat the first time on the stage. On the next run, though, with different blocking, the scene was to light up. The blocking was more spread out; the actors moved on the line more. This was a significant example of the importance of being prepared to change blocking arrangements once a play takes to the Globe stage.

Blocking work on 4.4 was another example of effective '3-D' staging. Pistol stands in front of the central opening, a rope stretched in a diagonal to the Boy who stands before the stage-left pillar. Le Fer enters cluching his longbow, at the stage-left entrance, and runs straight into the rope to be trapped by Pistol and the Boy. The stage business takes place in the central section of the stage. Pistol and Le Fer exit stage-right. The Boy speaks the final lines of the scene at the front of the stage, then exists through the central opening. The short, 24-line scene that follows (4.5) was done with spread-out blocking which, again, worked well from the sides of the stage. The Dauphin was brought forward to cross the front of the stage to deliver his lines to the Globe audience as though it were the French army he is pleading with:

> *Mort de ma vie*, all is confounded, all!
> Reproach and everlasting shame
> Sits mocking in our plumes
>   (*A short alarm*)
> *O mechante fortune!* Do not run away.

At 4.6 Henry enters stage-left, not through the central opening because the French prisoners, huddled in blankets, are standing with their backs turned in front of the central opening. The hangings are drawn across, then there is the sound of the prisoners being killed. Just before 4.7 there is the sound of a single scream offstage. The hangings are drawn back, and the dead body of the Boy lies in the central opening. Llewellyn and Gower enter stage-right. Stage hands drag the body backstage.

22 May: Third Day of Technical Rehearsals on Stage

More work on the underpinning of the stage trap. This was necessary to ensure that the sound of the actors' footsteps over the trap area would be the same as over all the other parts of the stage floor. First technical run 6–10 p.m.
Full run of the play to test technicals.

23 May: Back in the Rehearsal Room for Notes and to Discuss the Question of the Rushes

- It was generally agreed that the rushes were causing problems, but there was a willingness to keep trying with them.
- It was pointed out that the rushes would probably work better when they had worn down: after three weeks on the floor of the rehearsal room, the rushes had completely broken down and were now a more manageable size. Actors playing women said they had to lift up their crinolines which was awkward. One actor made the observation that Burbage would not have moved on rushes; another said that he got wet cold feet in thin leather shoes. Most of the company said they must feel at ease with the rushes. Richard Olivier commented that the actors tended to be 'bedded down' in them. Some of the actors felt that the rushes distracted them from being 'in' the scene; that they were too aware of 'clomping through the rushes'. It was decided to cut the rushes shorter and to water them just before each performance starts.
- There was much discussion about blocking of scenes, particularly 5.2, when Burgundy is on stage with Henry and Katherine. Different blocking was tried out to avoid long speeches being delivered by actors standing in one position.
- Matthew Scurfield asked about the question of rank in relation to Exeter bringing props on to the stage. It was decided to try alternatives.

26 May: First Dress Rehearsal, 7–10.30 p.m.; 27 May: Second Dress Rehearsal, 2 p.m.

The rushes were cut shorter so they looked better and were easier to walk on. The actors playing women said the rushes were much better, and have tried out walking on tip-toe, which also helps.

- A great many blocking ideas were tried out. At 3.5 Richard Olivier told the actors 'If you find yourself staying in the same place, I want you to move.' For 3.8, for the scene with the French on the eve of battle, the hangings in the central opening were drawn back on wooden poles to create the sense of the opening of a royal tent. The actors playing the French held goblets of 'wine' and emerged from the 'tent' as if digesting a fifteen-course meal.

- In 4.1 work on the blocking for Pistol's threat to the disguised King proved to be a fast lesson in finding out that 'proscenium arch' blocking is particularly ineffective for the Globe stage. At first, Pistol and Henry were standing without much movement, both facing the yard. The second time, they began to turn to each other, again with little movement. The third time they faced each other, with Pistol much more threatening with his sword and dagger, and continually moving towards the King. The Globe space encourages moving on the line and with actors facing each other to speak and react.
- A stool was placed on the stage on which the Dauphin would stand to deliver the beginning of his sonnet, and on which the Constable and Rambures would throw dice at the end of the scene.
- Blocking and movement for the 'leek' scene (5.1.) was experimented with, Pistol being knocked down twice by Llwellyn's 'truncheon', ending up with his head hanging over the edge of the stage as he is made to eat the leek.
- Matthew Scurfield, playing the Duke of York, could not hear his cue from the right entrance and he had to use the other entrance. This is important because it suggests that decisions about entrances and exits in the original staging may have depended on the practical consideration of whether or not an actor could hear his cue. The stage trap was still being worked on.

After the second dress rehearsal, the company met to discuss problems and difficulties. Mark Rylance said, 'We can run the story, it's the technicals that were a problem'. The actors expressed concern about not being able to hear the cues, particularly when there were 20 or so people backstage, with the result, as one actor said: 'I walked on too early, or too late.' Also there was concern about the time needed for the changes for the army costumes: these would need more work. The abiding preoccupation of the actors on the day of the second dress-rehearsal was: 'Will the technicals work tonight?'

7

The Play in Performance

First and Second Previews: 27 May, 7.30 p.m./ 28 May, 7.30 p.m.

The Audience Joins the Production

The audience participated in the performance to an even greater degree than audiences in the Workshop and Prologue Seasons. Experience had already shown how an audience newly liberated, highly visible, and energized by the Globe's spatial relations of building, stage and auditorium in the same light, can influence the playing of a scene. At the first preview performance of *Henry V* this empowerment of the audience and the energizing of the actors were reinforced. The groundlings in the yard made the most noise, especially in their responses to the French lords, who were greeted with progressively louder boos and hisses every time they came on stage. The first preview audience of each production at the new Globe includes the 'Penny Groundlings', the local residents who pay one penny to stand in the yard. Their responses are exhuberant. Coming offstage at the end of the performance, actors Christian Camargo (the Dauphin), Rory Edwards (Orleans) and Craig Pinder (Rambures) said they were completely astonished at the reaction – it was a little unnerving. Toby Cockerell (Katherine) was surprised at the cheers his character received when she first came on (3.5). She was greeted with wolf whistles. Henry and the English were cheered on every time they came onstage. A good number of the higher-paying seated playgoers in the galleries left their seats to join the groundlings standing in the yard. After the show, some of these playgoers said that they thought the groundlings were having more fun. Some did go back to their seats, more to rest legs than preferring the position in the auditorium. I noted: 'It is perhaps more accurate to describe some of the behaviour of the audience as a participation in the play rather than a response to it.'

At the time, it felt very much a manifestation of the feeling in the celebratory spirit of the first public performance in a newly built theatre, the culminating moment of a long struggle that had been finally won. The impulse on the part of the audience to take part in the event produced both deliberate and spontaneous responses. My notebook entry reads:

> Is this just contrived 'joining in'? Sometimes it seems manufactured, sometimes it's natural. Perhaps playgoing in an open playhouse simply provokes a "natural" desire to "manufacture" the response? And if it is contrived, does it matter? At moments when the audience is emotionally moved and goes quiet, its participation is as strong. The vocalized response and the quiet response are both prompted by the players in their fiction. And by the building itself? Schoolchildren, bikers covered in tattoos, babies a-piggy-back, a helicopter overhead trying to drown out Canterbury's tedious speech in 1.1(!) If an uninhibited, freewheeling audience becomes spell-bound by the fiction, Shakespeare was a better playwright than we thought.

28 May/29 May, After the First and Second Previews

Actors had found their cue lines difficult to hear backstage. Director's notes included:

1. Reminders to actors not to be stuck in a position for too long.
2. Entrances – actors have to allow time to come in and take up their positions to get the line delivered.
3. Actors were making positive use of the discovery space.
4. On the decision to show the three traitors, appearing one by one as their names are called, at the entrance doors and discovery space, during the Act Two Chorus: 'three corrupted men – / One, Richard, Earl of Cambridge, and the second/Henry, Lord Scroop of Masham, and the third/ Sir Thomas Grey, knight of Northumberland...' (22–5), the director and actors felt the audience treated the three as pantomime villains, and that a different approach was needed. It was suggested to show the three traitors in a tableau in the discovery space to 'keep the dramatic irony, without encouraging the audience to hiss and boo'.
5. There was a good deal of discussion about audience responses to the French characters – a progressively active hissing and booing. There was a need, it was felt, for the actors to be able to 'front

them out', speak more clearly, and learn ways of dealing with the audience, so that 'we don't lose the sense of the "whole", of the story; so we don't let a moment get pulled apart. We have to learn to control that.' Another view was that 'We have to go out open-minded. The audience have the right to respond any way they want.'

6. The director stressed the need for 'more volume upstage' and reminded actors that when they are downstage there are people 'behind' you (meaning the playgoers at the extreme sides of the stage on all three levels).

7. Richard Olivier emphasised 'the need to move on this stage'. Olivier also stressed the need for '*clarity*: Clearly some people aren't going to see everything, but they *hear* everything'. He reminded the actors of the 'forty or so people who don't see anything if you stay hidden behind a pillar', and said 'we owe something to them'.

8. It was suggested that some cork should be given to Henry so that he could black-up to help his disguise in 4.4.

Actors' responses to the first previews included:
'We acted as storytellers'.
'The place tells one how the story should be told.'
'The theatre tells us what to do.'
'The Globe tells you how to play it.'
'It tells you when you've gone too far, or not enough.'
'The audience – you get so much back from them. That's an experience I've never had.'
'The audience – there was so much listening.'
'The audience was less rowdy at the second preview.'
'There was a gentler energy at the second preview.'
'As if the audience wants to stretch every moment, to make the thing last longer.'

28 May: Rehearsals on Stage

- The actors practised looking up at the galleries as they played the scenes. Building debris was being cleared away. Electricians were at work.
- Tested trap and smoke device – it worked.
- Richard Olivier kept sitting and standing at the sides of the stage to monitor potential blocking of sightlines.

- The actors spent a lot of time rehearsing lines walking around the stage looking up and around the galleries. Olivier kept directing the actors to come to the front corners of the stage before the pillars.

Changes through the Run

'Changes through the run' is slightly misleading in the context of this Globe production, because it was not 'pre-set' to the extent that many theatre productions are. As we have seen, preparation in the rehearsal rooms was focused on flexibility in staging, with a deliberate willingness to make changes once the play was taken on to the stage. An awareness of the differences which the presence of the audience in the Globe space would make to the staging was also an important part of the rehearsal process. Responding to those differences meant that performance on stage was as much, sometimes more than, a process of experimenting and exploring as that of the rehearsal period.

Blocking

Not surprisingly, blocking was one of the most significant aspects of changes in staging. Responding to the demands of the configuration of stage and playgoers was a discovery process in itself and meant that the actors were experimenting with the possibilities of '3-D' playing until the last performances of the play. This was perhaps the most noticeable response of the actors to the presence of the audience surrounding them; part of what is meant by the sense they expressed after the two previews, about the theatre 'telling us how to play it'.

- There was a general trend towards longer diagonals through the run, using the depth of the stage as well as the breadth. Using the depth for diagonals was found to be effective in creating '3-D' playing.
- Another general trend was that of more playing upstage and in front of the *frons scenae*, particularly in scenes which emphasize the intimacy and unity of the English soldiers. This was an important result of the exploration of the stage's '3-D' possibilities: the playgoers at the sides of the stage in the galleries were made to feel more involved.

- Two characters speaking close together is not very effective. Standing further apart seems to make the communication more accessible to the audience.

- At moments when a character was left alone on stage to talk to the audience, the actor would tend to move round the stage more in order to be able to address different sections of the audience on the three different levels, and therefore to move on the line more. But see below . . . .

- An important development of the impulse to keep moving on the Globe stage is that, at moments when a character stands still to speak and looks at individuals in the audience, it is more effective for being delivered on one spot. This seems to be another example of how the production continues to develop once it is on the stage before an audience.

- There tended to be more spreading out, particularly with the use of positions in front of the two pillars on the corners of the stage when three or more characters were onstage.

- The pillars were used more for what would have been, on stages using controlled lighting, 'out of the spotlight' moments when the focus is on another part of the stage. For example, Williams, Bates and Court are grouped around one of the pillars 'hidden' from Henry's view, and Henry is hidden from their view before the disguised King is discovered in 4.1.

- The discovery of the dead Boy in the central opening was thought to be confusing to some sections of the audience: the playgoers at the extreme sides of the stage next to the tiring house wall and those in the 'Lords' rooms' in the balcony, in particular. It was decided that the Boy would stagger out of the central opening and die a few inches in front of it.

- The French in 3.8. played the scene more and more drunk through the run. Interestingly, the first time this scene was run in the rehearsal room the actors played it exceedingly drunk. In the final performances, the drunkenness became as extreme, sometimes more so when a section of the groundlings grew boisterous, as when it was played in the first rehearsal. This was one among several examples of the way in which the presence of the audience influenced how the actors would play a scene.

- The rushes were cut shorter and shorter, and were damped down with a large sprinkler before, and frequently during breaks in the performance.

8

Revelations and Discoveries

In a Hamburg garret I once saw a production of *Crime and Punishment*, and that evening became, before its four-hour stretch was over, one of the most striking theatre experiences I have ever had. By sheer necessity, all problems of theatre style vanished: here was the main stream, the essence of an art that stems from the storyteller looking round his audience and beginning to speak.... We were gripped by living theatre.... We were listeners, children hearing a bedside story yet at the same time adults, fully aware of all that was going on.... We never lost sight of being crammed together in a crowded room, following a story.

Peter Brook, *The Empty Space*[1]

Peter Brook's description of the power of what he called 'rough theatre' to conjure up a whole complex fictional world for an audience that becomes gripped by it and yet remains aware that it is listening to a story finds a parallel in the experience of *Henry V* playgoers at the Globe.

Two of the discoveries made at the *Henry V* performance can, I think, be justly termed revelations. They relate to the boy-actor playing a woman, and to the role of storytelling in the Globe space.

The Boy-Actor

A young man in the part of Katherine in *Henry V* in an open amphitheatre has shown very clearly that, as with any part, an actor who can convince you of the truth of a character will compel an audience to believe in the role. One of the most instructive aspects of research work on the production was to watch Toby Cockerell's characterization of Katherine develop from its flirty, rather stereotypical *idea* of how a young woman talks, moves, and behaves into the fully-realized, psychologically motivated and real character that he became. His Katherine was believable in the rehearsal studio before he started to wear practice skirts and wigs, just as the other actors playing soldiers were before they began to wear their armour.

116

Toby Cockerell's Katherine demonstrated that, as with any aspect of the power of fiction in drama to compel belief, it is possible for audiences to accept that what is before them on stage is a young woman. It seems such a naively obvious observation to make, but at a time when much Shakespeare criticism on the subject of the boy-actor has focused on the supposed homoerotic function of male actors playing women, it perhaps needs to be stressed that most, if not all, of the time, if a male actor plays a female role, the audience will take him to be a woman in any other role. Even when there are potentially self-reflexive allusions to the boy-actor behind the costume within the play, the allusion does not have to 'disrupt' audience-absorption in the story. For example, when Isabel, the French Queen, says in 5.2: 'Happily a woman's voice may do some good/ When articles too nicely urged be stood on', some playgoers would often register their 'knowingness' with a quiet murmur or chuckle because they knew 'behind' Isabel was a male actor, but this had no more effect on believing in the reality of the character than when Coriolanus tells the audience in an aside that he is 'like a dull actor'. The question of whether Katherine is played by a male actor or a female actor seems not to be a noticeable factor in audience responses. Twenty-two-year-old Cockerell himself was surprised that some playgoers did not know Katherine was being played by a man.

It was particularly valuable to discover that when actors were auditioning for the part of Katherine, it was felt that the voices of the teenage actors who tested for the role did not carry in the new Globe space. Future productions with young male actors with voices like that of Cockerell, playing women, will offer more insights into the functioning of the boy-players in early modern drama.

Storytelling
The Globe is pre-eminently a listening space, a place for telling a story. The *Henry V* actors, guided by the director, allowed the story to tell itself in a way that it is not normally possible when a production is concept- or design-led. There is no stage lighting to create mood, no technology to convey a sense of day or night, no directed lighting to give specific focus to characters. There are no stage properties to create a sense of place or an elaborate stage-set to provide a mimetic illusion. The play and the actors, and at times, the music, control the audience's imagination to an unusual degree.

The Audience

The contribution of the playgoers and their imaginations to performances of *Henry V* is inadequately described by the term 'audience response'. Even in the 1995 Workshop season with small capacity houses and actors reading from their texts, it was apparent that the actor–audience relationship would need to be redefined.

At *Henry V* performances the groundlings in the yard tended to dominate the reception of events on stage. They were the most vocal in the hissing and booing of the French, and the cheering of the English. It was impossible for the actors to ignore them, and also sometimes tempting for actors to 'work' the yard. Seated playgoers regularly left their more expensive positions in the galleries to join the groundlings because they felt they would be more involved. Actors quickly realized that they needed to find ways of playing 'through' the groundlings to reach other parts of the audience in the galleries. Impromptu by-play with playgoers would seem to need to be resisted more often than not. If the interaction between player and playgoers is allowed to interrupt the story, the fictional world is subverted and the play suffers.

The Actor/Role Relationship

As with our understanding of the effects of the boy-actor on the English Renaissance stage, traditional scholarship concerning the exact nature of dramatic illusion in Shakespearean theatre will have found reason to reassess some assumptions about the relationships between the extradramatic, the metadramatic and the staged illusion. Daylight and the proximity of the audience to the stage affects perception of the relationship between the actor and the role. It is a complex interplay in which the actor has to find ways of remaining within the fiction, telling the story, and directing out to a visible audience, engaging with them as both actor and role.

Rehearsals

A result of the artistic policy of trying to create working practices and relationships which encourage company work on the play in all its aspects to be a shared process of discovery was that actors in this production were given less strict parameters than is usually the case. Each production makes its own rules about how its work on the play will be approached, but what the space itself does is to provide a potential for a new kind of relationship to develop between actors and director. Richard Olivier was particularly keen to put this more open and collaborative approach into practice. The actors, accustomed to being given quite well-defined briefs from directors, found this kind of freedom – and shared responsibility – extremely fruitful and productive. Perhaps the most noticeable result was that the 'discovering' possibilities tended to have an 'open-ended' aspect to them, and so the quality of a discovery became as important as the discovery itself. Actors and director felt they were still discovering the play in significant ways well beyond the rehearsal period, and far into the performance period.

Blocking
Long diagonals across the depth and breadth of the stage help to create the three-dimensional staging required by the Globe space. In the rehearsal rooms anything that is fixed tends to have to be changed once it is put on to the stage. Moving on the line, and with actors facing each other to speak or react, is a natural way of playing the Globe space.

Entrances and exits
Overlapping entrances and exits worked very well, and are usually a necessary piece of staging at the Globe because it takes two or three lines for an actor to move from an entry door in the *frons* to the front of the stage. As was noted again and again, it is important to avoid moments when the stage is empty because the 'energy' in the theatre disappears; and apart from the strictly practical point of having to solve the problem of how long it takes to move across such a deep stage, overlapping exits and entrances help to make a production seamless. They also, of course, help to speed up performance time.

Use of the Stage Trap
As well as being used as the entrance to the 'mines' tunnelled under the walls of Harfleur, for the entrance of MacMorris and Jamy in 3.3, the trap was used as the 'tavern' from which Pistol and Mistress Quickly emerge to make their entrance in 2.1. The Boy delivered his speech at 3.3.24 from the trap, viewed 'waist-up' from stage level.

The Central Opening
This was used in different scenes for bringing on the English and French thrones: the English throne on a dais with canopy backed by cloth of estate and canopy showing the English arms, and the

French chair on a dais of state backed by a cloth of estate showing the French arms. These were placed in the '*locus*' or 'authority' position, centre-stage, a few feet from the central opening, a little way back from the 'line' in between the stage-posts.

The central opening was used to represent Henry's 'tent' and the French lords' 'tent' in their respective camps at Agincourt. The stage hands drew back the hangings for entrances and closed them after exits. The central opening was not used for the entrances of Henry and his men during the Harfleur scenes where it was used to represent the town walls and then the town gates, through which Henry is invited by the governor of Harfleur to take the town.

The potential for a hierarchy of exits and entrances which the central opening and the flanking doorways of the tiring-house offers can also be used to signify a 'downgrading' of status: in 4.5, when the French lords rail against the shame of their defeat, they exit by a side door.

Use of the Balcony
For stage action, the balcony was used for certain speeches: for instance, the French King exhorting his princes to bring '[Harry England] our prisoner' in 3.6. This was a good example of what is meant by the term 'listening theatre'. The use of the balcony for delivering rousing speeches spoken by an actor whose voice has the clarity to carry to all parts of the auditorium means that any play-goer in the audience who has a restricted view, or has difficulty focusing on the speaker because of the absence of lighting in the balcony, can follow the language. The musicality of the verse can be exploited to great effect when lines are delivered from the balcony. The governor of Harfleur delivered his speech to Henry and his men from there as he would have in the original staging. The balcony was used as the walls of Harfleur, and the central opening as the gates of the town. The balcony was not used, as it would have been in the original staging, for the besieging of the town where the English soldiers would have put scaling ladders against the balcony to climb up.

The balcony was used as a musicians' gallery (although there is no evidence for this at the Globe until 1609) for much of the time. There were no partitions in the stage balcony to separate the musicians from the audience. Two actors, Craig Pinder and Steven Skybell, dressed in undershirts and not in character, sang the *Te Deum* and *Non nobis* from the balcony at the end of 4.8.

An interesting effect was produced at the end of 2.4, when, from the stage, Exeter interrupts the French royal flourish playing on the balcony – effectively overriding the French King's order.

At 2.1.69 Mistress Quickly delivers her lines from the balcony urging Pistol, Bardolph and Nym to attend the dying Falstaff.

Actor Use of the Yard

There is no evidence that the yard was used for play action at the original Globe. For *Henry V* it was used for entrances and exits by the Eastcheap characters and Llewellyn at Harfleur (3.2); and for Pistol's final exit in 5.1.

Intervals

Actors found a noticeable difference after the intervals in the quality of the audience's attention. Everyone felt that the audience was much more responsive in the second half.

Interval-free performances (June 21, 24; July 8, 22) were, in general, popular with the actors. Richard Olivier thought it flowed better without a 15-minute interval in the middle. The actors said it felt quicker, which may sound like a matter of stating the obvious in one sense, but of course it could have *felt* slower if their energy levels were sagging and they were feeling the loss of a break. There were two-minute pauses between acts to allow for 'costume' changes. Performance time for interval-free performances was cut from three hours, 15 minutes, to three hours (although it lasted slightly shorter when it rained or longer when moments of actor–audience interaction were prolonged).

No systematic survey of audiences' opinions on interval-free performances has yet been carried out. One would assume that the groundlings in the yard would find it more hard-going than seated playgoers. It did seem to make a difference that the audience in the yard had easiest exits through the theatre-doors for the two-minute pauses and indeed, for going outside during playing. Also, as with performances with a 15-minute interval, the freedom of movement afforded to the groundlings, even simply knowing that you can move about whenever you felt like a change, or to get a different angle on the stage, greatly helped audience attention-span and willingness to put up with standing. A surprising number in my random and unscientific questioning of groundlings in the yard after interval-free performances had no objections to standing, including a 68-year-old man, who said it was fine; and a large number said they didn't leave the yard to get a drink or visit the loo because 'we were too wrapped up in it; we didn't want to miss anything'.

Acoustics

The solid oak with which the stage is now built made a remarkable difference to the acoustics. (In the previous season it was a temporary stage made of plywood and steel.) Voice Coach Jeannette Nelson found that the theatre's acoustics are very resonant: 'It isn't volume that is needed. Actors – male and female – have to use all their vocal skills: if they don't support their voices effectively, the voice is thin, and this is particularly evident if they don't use their full range of resonance.' The acoustics changed to a considerable extent when it rained. The actors felt as though they were having to speak through a thunderstorm.

Cues

The problem of actors being unable to hear their cues backstage has yet to be solved satisfactorily. No cue-lights were used, and one of the musicians had to listen to the play. The drummer learned 30 cues by heart. It is not possible to have an offstage prompter with the stage as it has been constructed, and more experiments will have to be carried out to find out whether the solid flanking doors should be removed, and hangings put in their place, or other alternatives. We don't know what actors did about hearing cues at the original Globe. Actor David Fielder has made the valuable point that with verse drama and the emphasis on storytelling, 'it's a question of passing on the energy at the end of the line. You have to say the end of the line at the right pitch – it's as though you're passing on the baton.'

Warming up the Audience

This was achieved by drumming backstage. At most performances, and to a lesser or greater degree, the strong rhythmic beat encouraged the audience to join in by stamping a foot, clapping hands, or, in the case of groundlings up against the stage, drumming with their hands on the edge of the stage.

Signalling the Start

With a theatre where there are no 'lights down' or 'curtain up' to signal the start of the show, the question of quietening the audience and gaining their attention has to be addressed. With *Henry V* the performance onstage began with staggered entrances of actors to position themselves in different parts of the stage, each playing a drum or beating the stage with a stave, so the start of the play followed naturally from the backstage music. The Prologue Chorus stood at the front of the stage, held his stave aloft to signal the music to stop, beat the stage with it with a resounding thud, and began to speak the Prologue.

The Weather and Performance-Time
Performance-times are speeded up when it's raining. Actor Toby Cockerell pointed out that the actors could sense the playgoers wanting them to play faster. Actors have to increase their volume when it is raining. But other kinds of climatic conditions affect sound. When the air is humid and oppressive, it has the effect of softening the vocal sounds. The level and volume which actors speak on one day, when it is clear, will not be enough on another, when the air is dense. A surprisingly large number of groundlings stood it out in the rain.

The Audience and Performance-Time
Audience responses – particularly laughing and the frequency of applause – often lengthened performance time by as much as 15 minutes.

Musicians
Another aspect of the artistic policy was to encourage a close relationship between the actors and musicians. Music was accorded a position of prime importance to the production.

Design
The experience of experimenting with the rushes was a good example of how playing the Globe space is able to produce research findings about original staging. The practical use of authentic production methods means that actors can provide what might be termed 'experiential evidence' to be weighed with archaeological evidence and academic scholarship.

Scene-Changes
Seamless scene-changes seemed to be suited to the Globe space – the audience concentrates on whoever is speaking next, and so props can be taken off while the action of the next moment is played without any serious distraction.

Period Clothing

The *Henry V* production recreated period clothing out of materials and dressmaking methods that were in use at the time of the original Globe. The intention was for actors to feel that they were wearing real clothes rather than the kind of theatrical costuming which tends to be made as 'one piece' with modern methods, materials and fastenings. For *Henry V*, most of the clothing was hand-stitched, including the undergarments, and the different parts of each outfit were fastened in original fashion. This posed some problems for costume changes because of the number of ties that needed to be fastened and unfastened which, of course, took more time than zips, velcro, and other modern methods, and suggested that some use of breaks would have been needed by the original players during performances when doubling parts.

Props and Furniture

It was not possible for stage design and stage management to construct and make everything with original materials, tools and methods because of budget restrictions, and the company would also have liked to have been able to carry out research into authentic methods of making props and furniture, such as the 'tun' of tennis balls brought to the English court from France. The cannon fired in the gable was borrowed from the replica of *The Golden Hinde*.

Playgoers Fainting

An unusually large number of playgoers fainted during performances at the new Globe. Research is being carried out to find out more about this phenomenon. Extreme heat and the colourful *frons scenae* have been put forward as possible main causes.

WARM-UPS AND OTHER THINGS THAT HELPED

As you would expect, much – perhaps all – of what was found to be helpful in preparing the play for the Globe stage is interrelated. It will also become evident that the following ten of the most notable aspects of what helped are dependent to a great extent on the whole company's capacity to embrace working relationships and practices that encourage creative interaction and mutual discovery of the text – and, of course, to embrace a visible, highly communicative audience.

- Not 'pre-setting' the production in the rehearsal room.
- Trusting the story, and trusting the theatre-space to support the storytelling.
- Accepting the challenge of having the 'crutches' of lighting and design taken away.
- A great willingness to be flexible about blocking and to expect to make changes once the play was tried on stage.
- Allowing time and space in the preparation schedule for the development of the exploration and discovery process. For example, the eve-of-battle scene 4.1 was discussed, improvised and worked on again and again. Everyone felt that so complex a scene needed however long it would take to do justice to it. To have the opportunity to let the whole preparation process to grow from the story was felt to be of central importance in preparing the play for the Globe space.
- Imagining, while in the rehearsal rooms, what it was going to be like to play in the Globe space, and this meant imagining a visible audience as well as imagining acting on the deep, wide stage and its pillars. It was important to remember: the trap when it was open (!); it's dark; you have to move quietly backstage because of having to hear cues, and you mustn't cough – ironically, all the kinds of restrictions imposed on audiences in traditional proscenium-arch theatres with a darkened auditorium. It is the actors in the fictional world on the stage that are, at times, silent and motionless.
- Giving thought to the possible responses of the original audiences of the play. This is true of any Shakespeare production in any other theatre-space. At the Globe it is perhaps more natural to be prompted to think in this way because of the physical configuration of actor and audience in that theatre. Throughout the preparation of this history play, there kept emerging the question of whether the play should be reflecting Henry's time or Shakespeare's time. Apart from considering the play's obvious anachronisms such as Pistol, where his name is given to a character that was supposed to be living in a time before such firearms were invented, or the play's allusions to contemporary events such as the imminent return from Ireland of the Earl of Essex, a twentieth-century production of *Henry V* that is following an 'authentic brief'

will be aware that for the original audiences, the Battle of Agincourt was England's last famous military victory. To recover something of the knowledge about the play's events which the original Globe players and playgoers would have brought to a performance of the play, reference was frequently made to modern historians' studies of the battle of Agincourt and brought into discussions of how to play the military scenes.

A good deal of time was devoted to discussions about Canterbury's speech on the Salic Law in 1.1. The director and actors felt it was useful to be aware of its significance for original audiences who were living during a reign in which the dynastic consequences of Elizabeth I marrying a foreign prince had been a hotly debated issue. A present-day audience would not come to the play with such knowledge, but it was felt that such knowledge and understanding informed the playing of the scene and by extension the audience's understanding.[2]

- Actor's warm-up on stage – both voice and movement. Both the Voice Coach and the Movement Coach stressed that a good warm-up session was essential at the Globe. Richard Olivier made the point several times to the actors during the rehearsal period of *Henry V* that they could not expect to go onstage and then raise their energy levels. 'You have to have your energy levels up at a certain level when you go on.'

- Using the space just behind the central opening in the tiring-house for the psychological warm-up.

- Allowing time in both the preparation and the performance schedules of the play for the company to get together so that each member had the opportunity to talk about how the whole process was working out for him as an individual and in the group.

Part III
New Voices
from the Playhouse

Toby Cockerell, Actor: Katherine/the Boy in *Henry V*; Stephen/ Mistress Brook in *A Chaste Maid*

The first time on stage was very scary, but then once you started, it was quite reassuring, because the space felt quite friendly. But it was still frightening. The audiences at the Globe were different. I got a big cheer when I came on as Katherine. It threw me a little.

I thought it was going to be impossible to do Katherine. I didn't know how I was going to tackle it. After two weeks doing the scenes a few times it began to make sense. It wasn't really up to scratch until we went onto the stage. Even then, we were still working out blocking. It was very unplanned. It worked because we were free to develop. We weren't told, 'This is what you must do' and 'musn't do'. It developed.

Not having seen anyone perform on the stage before with a full audience, we didn't know how it was going to work. Everyone was given a chance to make mistakes so that we could see for ourselves why something didn't work. It was always developing right up until the last three weeks of the run. It's different from playing at the Barbican Theatre. There, you can't see anyone. You can tell everyone's listening, but there's just a big blackness out there in front of you. The Globe stage seemed so much bigger. In a way it's easier in a traditional theatre. At the Globe the freedom of the audience and the actors means it's different nearly every night. Because blocking wasn't set, every influence offstage influenced the way we played onstage. So when we started doing *Chaste Maid* our work on that play affected what we were doing with *Henry V*.

If it was raining it made a huge difference. When it was raining, windy or cold, you felt the audience wanted it to be quicker. They were more impatient, or they would lose interest. The play would move much faster in the rain. With some things that meant an improvement; some not. Interval-free performances of *Henry V* felt quicker.

One of the main things about rehearsing Katherine was that after two weeks I had the real costume to try out. It was so precisely made it forced me to move in a certain way – I would just glide across the floor. You can't walk fast at all. There was lots of restriction in the chest, I found it hard to breathe.

It would have been so easy to slip into a pantomime feeling. I didn't want Katherine to be a humorous 'girlie' character. I tried to imagine being a real princess in those circumstances at the time, instead of being a boy-actor dressed up as a girl. We did a lot of work on the last scene. The English court was aggressive, powerful; the French court accepting, trying to keep face. I'm so glad the French weren't made to end up being the baddies in this *Henry V*. Katherine was clever – it was a political situation to save France. She would have had discussions with Burgundy about the situation explaining why the marriage was important to France. She is still fighting for France to the end of the war. She's resolving the situation. She gets Henry to drop the heroic warrior act and he realises he's not good at talking to a woman. We decided the last scene must not be a cliché with a happy ending. Having the French king as the Epilogue was perfect.

Katherine's costume was visually stunning. She was so completely different from my other character, people didn't realize I was the Boy. Some people didn't realise it was an all-male cast. It shocked a lot of people. I had to forget all about pantomime. After a while it became quite comfortable, I had a long time to think about it. Katherine was one of the first to be cast. I really didn't know what was going to happen. It probably helped that I'm not established in the theatre, and didn't have a huge career to risk. It was OK to make mistakes. It was easy to feel you could do something wrong in rehearsals and on stage. We had lots of freedom – it's absolutely essential to make mistakes here.

The cast got on really well with each other. It gave the play what I call a 24-hour feel. It's such a lovely feeling when you're on the stage looking down. It looks like there's hardly anybody there. But when you're the audience, it's a huge stage, especially when you're a grounding. When actors come to the front of stage they look like *giants*. The audience was no threat whatsoever. The wolf-whistling when I first came on as Katherine was positive. It gave me confidence. For the first few performances – when the French were booed and hissed at, we thought, how insensitive to shout over the actors' lines. But the actors learned to wait, to let them boo, then say the line. I had mixed feelings about the time a group of schoolchildren was disrupting the performance. After all, it must have been that noise-level in Shakespeare's day. A worse level, I should think. The kids were having fun. At the time it would have been like that. The actors would have had to find a way of engaging the audience that weren't paying attention. They must have had such a *hard* job – the kind of crowd you get at a football match. It takes a different kind of actor to go on that stage; a different style of acting. To control that kind of crazy audience must have been very difficult. But I'm surprised we had any kids at all. We had school-groups at nearly every matinée. It was amazing, the sheer amount of them that wanted to listen.

For the death of the Boy, we had a discussion about whether we should have him there at all as we weren't showing any of the battle-scenes; no violence; no battles; no blood. When the Boy was dead inside the central opening, the audience were confused – they didn't all know who it was. Then I did it so that I would stagger through the opening and then die in front of the opening. It was mayhem backstage at that moment. I screamed – of course, the text never says the Boy is the character who dies. That was our intervention.

But almost everything we tried that wasn't in the text we would do and decide it didn't work. We would say, 'Stop. No. Take it back to the text, to what is written.' Everything came out of the text – it was already there. It grew out of what was already in the text. What was being said, and how it was being said. It just comes to life on that stage.

The play's so well written. Often with Shakespeare you try to make the play more for a modern audience. I don't think the Globe needs to do that at all. As close to the 'original' is best. You don't know how they did it. Were they better storytellers than modern-day actors? He wouldn't have written such brilliant plays if the actors hadn't been brilliant.

There's something really strong about having the audience every-where around you. The Romans with their Colosseum, the Greeks with their amphitheatres – they were all in the round – it gives some special kind of energy. Sitting at the sides, in the balcony, standing around the stage – you can see everybody else's reaction. There are lots of practical things at the Globe which help us as actors. You can see everyone. If you take in the audience as a whole you realize every single person has the same expression. Mass expression! If they're confused, every face will have an expression of confusion on it. When they laugh, they all laugh at the same moment. When I was not speaking and could spot anyone who was not listening, I would automatically home in on them – they knew and would be embar-rassed. They knew you were looking at them. But what happens between the actors and audiences is not pantomime. It's a serious fantasy, a fairy tale with truth.

Mark Rylance, Actor: Henry in *Henry V*; Allwit in *A Chaste Maid*
Aural storytelling skills are very pertinent to acting, directing,

designing and composing at the Globe. In fact, the aural story is the medium for everything, and anything that gets in the way of deep involvement in the story greatly diminishes the unique ability of Shakespeare's plays and space to work to their full potential.

I begin to recognize the added potential of the Globe space as a medium particularly conducive for fostering the catalyzing of Shakespeare's marriage, and opposition, of thought and emotion. Thoughts are experienced within a human emotional context more powerfully in this amphitheatre architecture than in a proscenium design. I conjecture that this may be to do with the heavier dependence on sound and hearing as a medium rather than vision and sight. The Globe stage-decorations seem to be utterly baffling to some people's eyes, and others don't even notice them once the play is under way. I understand the eye has always been connected with the intellect and head, and the ear connected with the emotions and heart or chest area. I also notice that the emotional experience for an audience is both individual and collective at the same time. I have never felt such emotional responses to a Shakespeare play like *Henry V* from a modern audience. It seems to me that darkness divides and isolates an audience. Also the physical activeness of the body whether standing or seated on a bench at the Globe is a quite different state for the heart and mind. The elements add to an awakened and sometimes drenched sense of the physical body. In a Renaissance Hermetic context, the four bodies (physical, emotional, intellectual and collective spirit) seem to be considered in the design, or at least the effect, of the Globe. None are encouraged to be passive.

All work in the Globe benefits from a love and understanding of counterpoint, or antithesis. From the actor's use of ideas and sounds in a line, to the relationship between the actor and groundling. Everything will flourish with Shakespeare when we move near to his passion for antithesis. Venus and Adonis every morning and evening!

As actors, we need to encourage and develop the audience's ability to play along with us. This is a very new experience for audiences, one they may only remember through Pantomime or Proms events. Their responses are not always sincere or involved. Many are shy and unused to expressing themselves in a public place and so they fall into received patterns of response. All this can be said about us actors too, of course! All the world's a stage and all the men and women merely players.

Rhythm in the speech and play, which is to do with a musician's awareness of the most suitable tempo and accent, is also, I think, crucial to the emotional quality of the storytelling in the Globe. Live music replaces lighting and set as a very expressive part of play at the Globe. While not convinced what role music played in original performance, I know it is extremely effective in the new Globe. Sound is a more powerful tool in staging at the Globe than sight.

William Russell, Actor: French King/ Erpingham in *Henry V*; Tutor in *A Chaste Maid*
It's very different from all the theatres I've ever worked in. Even when I've worked in the round I've never had this wall of people so near and yet so far with the sea of groundlings all around you. I love the unexpected and the way in which the audience *always* seems to be with you. It's like a sea – they move with you. It's something to do with the amount of wood in the building, I think, and also this strange paradox that you feel almost a sense of shock with all those people around you, but when you go out there you have an intimacy with them which you don't have in other theatres; and this manifests itself very quickly.

The other thing is it is an actor's space. It's very, very much an actor's space. The actors feel relaxed in it. Just as the audience is liberated, so in the same way the actors are liberated. You feel a sense of freedom and excitement which I'm sure conveys itself to the audience and seems to come back to you, so you're double-charged all the time. This is a tremendous feeling for an actor and I've never felt it so vividly, even playing in the round and in the open air. It's something to do with this wall of people in front of you and that little patch of blue up there and the thatch and the wood, the sights and sounds of everyday life from the river and the sky all combining to give you a unique sense of belonging. Also it's the fact that the audience can become very still *and* they can be noisy, vociferous and always spontaneous. But that, in a way, helps you, and I quite like it when they're buzzy and noisy and booing and hissing. I don't like it when it's obviously manufactured and artificial but when it happens spontaneously then I really do like it. I think that's perhaps the key to the whole experience, and that's what it is for an actor here in the Globe, this living link with the audience. You play with them, and they with you.

You move on the stage in a very different way from a proscenium-arch stage. You can almost catch yourself by surprise because if you turn sharply you realize that there are other people seeing you who didn't see you before, because they're almost behind you. And sometimes they are really behind you, and they're all at different levels. The theatre forces you to make contact with them all. This is why all the questions about the pillars and the height of the stage itself are relatively unimportant. So long as the audience can hear, they maintain the link with the play. It's what they *hear* that they react to. And they do hear. I've watched the audience listening, and *I'm* listening in a new way to the other actors on the stage.

When some of the audience were very boisterous – if somebody was shouting a lot, I'd 'answer' him, I looked directly at him. I don't think it's anything to do with pantomine. I think that description is absolutely false. There's a link much more with the *commedia dell'arte* tradition.

The building itself is a stroke of genius. They *did* know what they were doing in those days, the people who built the theatres. Shakespeare and Burbage got it right. It's an absolute masterstroke. And as you play Shakespeare in the space that he created you marvel at the construction of his plays afresh with a new-born clarity.

How much can you direct in the sense which we have grown accustomed to directors directing Shakespeare? I don't know. What we need are people who've played the space and can talk about it and assess it, actors who are aware of all these things. From a designer's point of view there's a limited number of things you can do on that stage. You can't call up all the wizardry of modern stage-lighting. Most of the props in the armoury of the modern director are unusable. It is the actor who must create the magic on Shakespeare's stage.

I have a strong feeling that the Globe theatre could take more musicality in the actual speaking of the verse – which is difficult for modern actors to do. I don't ask for a return to great sonorous voice-work, but a sense of the music and the rhythms and the poetry, can be employed and explored with more daring and courage.

David Fielder, Actor: Llewellyn/ Le Fer in *Henry V*; Davy in *A Chaste Maid*
The shock of the first night – it felt as if we were all at a football match. We all anticipated that there would be something different about playing at the Globe but not something quite as exciting, and ... what's the world I want? – *ennobling*.

In the process of acting it had a very different feeling about the relationship between the spoken word and movement – you move and speak at the same time. In modern theatres we're not encouraged to move on the line.

The difference from playing other theatres is at the Globe it's a question of giving to the audience more, you have to open out much more than when you're in a closed box, in a controlled environment. You can still play intimate scenes, but you can't be too close. You don't have to shout, it can be very gentle. Clarity is important, you can pull it in quite small, the sound. You have to listen to the audience, know when to give time to their responses.

The yard? I'm quite sure the original actors wouldn't have played in the yard – it produced too many problems, and we were dealing with a much smaller capacity than the original yard held, today we live in a far more sophisticated society – a lot of niceness goes on in the theatre. You have to shout when you're playing in the yard, whereas you don't have to shout on the stage. I actually adored using the yard. The audience become part of it, and it becomes part of the audience. But I wouldn't think in the original Globe the actors used the yard.

We had so much freedom with our director that we could change our decisions once we got on to the stage. We tried lots of different blocking for most of the scenes. For example, where Llewellyn greets the King about the bridge, I greeted him downstage right, half crossed upstage when he went upstage left. I needed to find a place to stand by the time Montjoy comes on. After trying out many different types of blocking, we ended up with Llewellyn starting on the other side of the stage. It's a question of hot spots and cool spots. In that scene I needed to find a hot spot to say my lines, then end at a cool spot and avoid the hot spot, so that Montjoy could enter and deliver his lines from a hot spot.

My Chorus for Act III was always different, at every performance. I like playing in the round. I didn't worry that there were people at the sides and behind me. I didn't mind that. I like backs, I like giving the audience my back. One of the reasons I preferred the no-interval performances is that I like people having a choice to decide whether they want to have a wee or a drink, or stay and watch! If you start worrying that when someone leaves to go and get a drink that it's because you're a dull actor, that would be daft. It's part of the freedom and excitement of the place. I would mind in a closed box theatre, though. But at the Globe, it's more like the vast auditoria

I've played in China where there are 2000 people and the playgoers are coming in and going out all the time.

Hearing cues was a problem sometimes. In *Chaste Maid*, for example, people had trouble hearing cues when there was a band playing backstage. But with verse drama, and the emphasis on story-telling, it's a question of passing on the energy at the end of the line, certainly at the end of a scene. You have to end the line at the right pitch – it's as though you're passing the baton.

If an actor coming to play for the first time at the Globe were to ask me what to prepare for I'd probably say that I think the best thing would be if they're in good condition – physically and voice-wise. The space needs *energy*.

David Lear, Actor: Gloucester in *Henry V* ; Dick/Nurse/Waterman in *A Chaste Maid*

The audience are exposed. Five hundred – one-third of the audience – are standing, and that creates a different atmosphere. Standing up against the edges of stage, they're linked to the stage. On stage you feel that you're acting not *to* an audience, but acting *with* an audience. It's a much stronger connection than you achieve anywhere else. They become a part of what you're doing.

Also, being in the round – it's not strictly in the round, but thrust, you feel that some of your audience are behind you. The audience is on three sides. And the pillars – obscuring a lot of view – not just the pillars on stage but with people sitting behind pillars in the galleries, this restricts view. So it becomes more of a *listening* theatre. For the actor, it creates a tendency to want to move, to want to create space. When people are actually listening it creates a different kind of energy. The actor has a different kind of attention and awareness – *at all times*. What becomes really important is how to play the moment, even when you're not speaking.

Nothing about the theatre bothers me at all. I find the whole place very embracing. There is something about the whole theatre that is warm and welcoming – not like a proscenium-arch theatre. There is no fourth wall. It's interesting that a few times it's been some of the audience who have put the fourth wall back – like the time when there was a group of schoolchildren shouting, talking to each other loudly and it was difficult to carry on playing.

At the Globe, you have no lights. You have very little sound. You have no stage effects – and because the audience is actually there in front of you in full view, the only thing you have to work on is the audience's belief. Unless you start believing it's very difficult to keep yourself within that world. You can't do that when people are shouting and jeering. But when the audience is cheering and booing and getting engaged with the show it works really well. When they're in that yard they have different perceptions. As actors we musn't forget the people in the galleries. You must play to the galleries. The yard can easily be held. It's the people in the rest of the audience that need to be involved. If you try to get them and they're held, you'll hold the groundlings twice as much.

Nick Fletcher, Actor: Jamy/Bedford in *Henry V*; Sims/Mistress Bun in *A Chaste Maid*

Joining the Globe Red Company for the Prologue season was my first professional theatre job. I'm used to dark theatre from the university productions I've done. The one thing about the Globe that is more different from anywhere else? Being able to see people's faces is the practical answer, but more vaguely the whole atmosphere is totally different from a traditional theatre. When you can actually look into people's eyes, something different happens about your acting; it makes you act differently. There is more a relationship going on rather than it simply being a presentation.

The Globe space makes me feel better at acting in that I feel much happier about being present and losing myself totally in a pretend idea of another character. Maybe it's because I'm not so experienced so far, but I've found it much easier to do that and occupy other people's heads here than I've done anywhere else. The audience is more engaged in what I'm doing. When you have five hundred people standing proud right in front of you, who want something from you, and want to share something with you, you are aware of the expectation they are feeling. I really think that that affects you differently from squinting out at a lot of grey silhouettes who you don't feel any affinity with. For the audience it is different too. When you look into the eyes of an actor and that actor looks into your eye at the same time you should be aware at that point that you're actually watching an actor in a role playing a part in a fictional world, but it doesn't break the spell. It depends on how much anyone in the audience wants to take part, feel involved, and if they do, want to feel a part of it, then suspension of disbelief and all of that doesn't really come into question because everybody's pretending – the audience have got to contribute as much for it to work.

I'm guessing, but on the strength of the look on people's faces in the audience during Act IV of *Henry V* they're really there, their imagination is running riot. It was such a surprise to come on to the stage. We didn't know what to expect. I think it would help if we could rehearse on the stage say one day a week from the beginning of the preparation period.

The rushes I found a terrible problem all along. I appreciate why they're there, but they're very difficult to walk on; very slippery when you're running: especially when I went on to find the Boy dead or when carrying heavy things. It's extremely difficult to stay upright at speed with 40lb of iron on your shoulders waving a sword around. I didn't find that the costumes that I was wearing were forcing anything on my physicality. You do adopt certain attitudes. One of the first things I was keenly aware of about my Bedford costume was that *it was worth so much money and so much effort and time* that had gone into it, that I did feel quite princely putting it on and the fact that every little detail is correct, I suppose reinforces that feeling. The main thing that I found though was that the quick changes are very involved because you're doing a lot of tying up of knots, fiddling with bits and pieces, separating the different parts – mostly loops – it's quite a frenzy taking them on and off if you're in a hurry.

Rory Edwards, Actor: Orleans/Burgundy/Michael Williams in *Henry V*; Sir Walter Whorehound in *A Chaste Maid*
It's very difficult to describe what is different about the experience of acting at the Globe. It's a very complex question, and the trouble is, if you start to try to analyse it you have to start talking about things like 'a higher consciousness' which can sound crap. But I would say that I'm glad that whatever chemistry it is, it actually works.

Before we opened everyone was still unsure about how it would all work in that space in front of an audience. But it soon stopped being a personal, individual experience. You felt, as an actor, part of the whole project – the architecture, the audience, the company. There's something strangely liberating about the Globe, and to the actors who will be coming to play here I would say it will enhance them as an actor. And the same goes for directors and designers.

The clearest thing we found as actors was the level of communication with the audience. It's not just the fact that you can see them, not just the daylight. It's to do with the actual generation of energy in the circle within the building. It actually allows you to feel involved in the performance. As one of the ushers said, 'I feel part of the play.' In modern theatres, a modern black box, in the darkness, it is mainly about separation. At the Globe there's a sense of something opening up in the hearts and minds of the actors and audience. And it seems to be something, an atmosphere, that's created by the people involved in the project, which is to do with the idea of the continuity of theatre. And that has to involve a spiritual dimension. There is a bridge between Shakespeare and now, and it shows we haven't completely succumbed to the mechanistic world of film and technology.

John McEnery, Actor: Pistol in *Henry V*; Sir Oliver Kix/ Mistress Tool in *A Chaste Maid*
It was absolutely phenomenal to play the first season at the Globe. It was plain sailing on open seas. Mark (Rylance) was an inspiring captain at the helm, and Richard (Olivier) was so good at giving us the freedom to try things out. The endeavours of everyone involved in all parts of the theatre were cohesive. It's hard to define it exactly, except you were aware of the uniqueness of the experience – it was original to all who took part – the audience, the players, the academics all sharing it for the first time.

I haven't been used to playing among an audience, and it was disconcerting in the opening week to come through the yard. The groundlings could be alarmingly distracting unless you gave a very firm purpose to everything you were doing. But after a while this became less unsettling. You need a strong voice for the Globe. One of the treats for me was to get to play the Act V Chorus – that teetering on the edge of the character was a surprise.

Richard Olivier, Director: *Henry V*
When I first saw the Globe when I came to see *Two Gentlemen of Verona* in the Prologue season, it took my breath away. I didn't expect it to look so real, so packed out. Once you were inside there was a feeling of rightness about it. It would take a long time to figure out how to use it, but there was something magical about it right from the beginning.

My first reaction to the idea of directing *Henry V* was initially one of fear: How the hell do we try and work with it? But I felt that as long as there was a kind of truth to the story-telling, the building would support that. One of the difficult times came was when we were figuring out the design of it, the concept. And every time we came up with an idea – it felt good or looked good for about three days or a week, and then we realised that a design concept is not helpful. For us, for the *Henry V* we were doing, we didn't want clutter, we didn't want things getting in the way. Before we started rehearsal I think we were planning four stools, two different sized tables, two daises, two thrones, a sail for the dock, and various other bits and pieces and gradually as we went through we just found the design naturally eroding. Almost every time we did a scene once we'd done with furniture we'd say all right let's try and do it without, and every time we did it without, the scene was better.

In the rehearsal room we started the traitor scene I think at one point as an official ceremony with seven stools presenting it as an award ceremony to the soldiers on the dock. We did it a couple of times then took the stools away to see what happens when you stand up. We went for that. For me, the ideas were getting in the way of pure narrative, of what was going on, especially with *Henry V* which has such a powerful narrative drive, such a good story that the less you get in the way of it, the better.

The relationship between the actors and the groundlings can make those in the galleries feel excluded, so it depends how it's done; it depends on what measure of awareness it's done with on the part of the actors. In one performance, an actor was playing so much to the groundlings, interacting with them that it was actually getting in the way of the story, so that the groundlings were enjoying the effect they were having on the actors. The actors were able to pull it back to a good measure so that there was a rapport with the groundlings that wasn't self-indulgent, not getting in the way of the story.

It's not like pantomime – there are many different things the audience respond to. One of my favourite moments in the whole season was watching a group of 15 year-old schoolboys. They were chatting among themselves, but then when it got to Agincourt they were all standing up against the stage, elbows on the stage and totally spellbound.

I don't know, but I have a feeling if a new play was written for the space modern language here could be remarkable. It would have to be written for the building, to encompass the building and work on the audience's imagination. We seem to have been training writers for twenty years to get more and more realistic and less and less imaginative and this is the kind of building that's going to demand imagination. Because of the daylight, of course it's not Denmark, but you do believe it – the playwright and the actors make you believe it. Occasionally you're more in the play than knowing it's a play but the ability to hold the two opposites together actually gives it this magic. It also gives you a choice: 'Do I want to be an outside observer or do I want to be a participant?' And I think the ground-lings are more naturally drawn to being participants, although a lot of people who sat told us they do feel that sense of participation. I think it's being outdoors, being in slightly uncomfortable seats, having distractions around you. You see people – the first three times a plane comes over they all look up, and they realise 'Oh yes that's a plane it's flying across.' Then the next time a plane flies over they realise they have a choice. They either look up again, or say, 'Well I know what that is, well actually I'm more interested in this [what's happening on stage].' So they keep the focus through the distraction. And I think it's to do with the shape of the circle, which is something we did deliberately in the rehearsal room. A circle is inclusive by its nature. No one is left out. As soon as you're in a confrontational proscenium-arch-type setting you've got an up-and-down situation, whereas with a circle there's only up. The stage is in some way connected with the audience.

We drew on experience of working with myth, fairy tales and using Shakespeare as a myth in workshops. I've often wondered, Why do I never completely buy any of these films that are made about a myth or a fairytale?' It's really because they show too much. As soon as they *show* a magical experience, it's always less than what you could have imagined it would be. The battle of Agincourt is told, not shown. You never see the battle. You hear about it. You imagine a battle; imagine you see somebody on stage.

I think the academic involvement in the Globe project, is part of what this place does – it's a unique opportunity for academics and practitioners getting together and having an exchange. I was actu-ally quite nervous about the academic involvement in the begin-ning. David Freeman [director of *The Winter's Tale*] and I were both expressing to each other a concern at having an apparently observ-ing eye in the rehearsal room and actors feeling they were being judged. We underestimated the ability of the actors to perform in front of an audience. For the actors and for me to have a resource available to answer questions, that was very valuable.

For the authentic brief, the way I took it was that we would, as a production, undertake to explore certain authentic production methods or styles. Not that we were trying to make the whole thing as it would have been in the 1500s but that we would – as Mark as Artistic Director and leading actor very much involved, and with Jenny [Tiramani, the Designer] – decide in advance what things we were going to be authentic with and would allow a kind of breath of modern air and hopefully come in and reinvigorate those authentic methods.

The drumming as a heart-beat? That had something which nobody in the Elizabethan world would have heard, but it was something I felt would give a life and a lift-off point to the production.

There were a number of reasons for splitting the Chorus the way we did. Within the play we wanted to set up the idea that it was a company of actors telling a story – a company of storytellers. We couldn't afford an actor to play just the Chorus. A number of well-known actors asked if they could play it. But we couldn't afford to do that. Then we considered having one character play the Chorus throughout. But that would have put too much emphasis on one character of the play. Once you know that can't happen, you're then going to give a very big influence on the play to the character who is playing the Chorus. It would draw attention to the sense of one character more than any other character when what we were trying to do was to draw attention more to the story. What we could do is draw attention to a certain character in each act, a character who has a certain impact in each act, an act in which they have a role. It developed from there, really. Mark didn't want to be the first Chorus, but I felt that since the speech is welcoming the audience to the building, Mark should say it. It should, of course, have been Sam [Wanamaker] speaking the Prologue, but failing Sam's physical presence it seemed to us that the Artistic Director was the appropriate person to do it.

I hope the Globe's evoking a new kind of energy – and it could have evoked a very old kind of energy. It's very hard to know how to transfer what happens here into another theatre because it's so different, but that's part of the magic.

The Globe shows you don't have to be in the dark. It seems to be that in modern theatre, a tendency and temptation is to let technology to do more and more of the audience's work for them. First, you put people in the dark, so they're not worried who's sitting next to them. You put up a beautiful set so they don't have to imagine where they are – the set has told them where they are – and then you light it in such a way that you tell people *who* to look at. Actors know they're on show all the time on the new Globe stage. It's more intimate and intense. The energy level of the audience is just different, partly because of the building and partly because of the people who work here are giving rather than taking, primarily – there's not a lot of ego around here. There aren't people making their names here or trying to become well-known. People feel as if they are in the service of the building.

I don't think I can draw any general lessons for other directors, but I know for myself it has reinforced the belief that the play's the thing. Personally I'm not good at mucking about with, and tarting up, some piece of writing I don't really believe in, but I love trying to draw out the best of a piece of really good writing. I think this is a space that allows that to happen in a very pure way. I'm sure there will be lots of concepts and ideas that will work in this space, but for me, approaching it for the first time, it was really important not to prejudge it and it was actually about stripping away and leaving the toolbox outside the theatre, even at the risk of almost being a bit dull. There was a sense in which I just wanted to allow what was there to come out and not dress it up. To see what *is* there.

Craig Pinder, Actor: MacMorris/ Rambures/ Cambridge/ Court in *Henry V* ; Robert/ Parson/ Waterman in *A Chaste Maid*
I first came to see the theatre, before I knew I was going to be in the Opening season, to see *The Two Gentlemen of Verona*. Acoustically there were problems – the stage wasn't finished then. I thought it was exciting. Then, when I knew I was going to be playing the space, it was frightening too. It wasn't until the previews of *Henry V* [playing to audiences] that all that fear went. I found it very welcoming, that space. It didn't feel awkward to move on the stage; it felt quite natural. Standing as a groundling looking at the stage, it seems a huge, grand stage. It is a very different perspective from the one we get on the stage when we're acting on it. The audience are closer to you than in traditional theatres. I have to say there is a tendency for actors to play out front – the proscenium-arch view. When we had a lot schoolkids in the yard who were talking among themselves, it wasn't that it was threatening, just that we felt we weren't able to do our job. It made it very difficult to project beyond them to the rest of the audience. I never really felt the audience threatening. I think we found it a little difficult at first to adjust to people responding in the way they did. You're not used to that. It's very different from the way Shakespeare is usually

received: when people are in the dark, you laugh, but you don't shout out.

The audience response when we came out as the French in *Henry V* did feel over the top. Maybe we thought it was contrived some of the time. There is lots more potential energy when the audience is standing, and that generates energy on to the stage. The Globe seems to be able to absorb all kinds of energy. Basically it's a listening space. My feeling about the 'authentic brief' we had for the play is the greatest plays ever written were written in this kind of theatre.

Jeannette Nelson, Voice Coach: *Henry V, A Chaste Maid, The Winter's Tale, The Maid's Tragedy*

I found the experience in the Opening season very exciting. We tried to give the actors as much opportunity as possible to prepare their voices for the demands of the new theatre. This included voice classes throughout the rehearsal period as well as warm-ups before performances. Unfortunately, as the theatre was still being finished during the first rehearsal period, we were unable to have time in the space before the technical rehearsals began. With the second two plays [*A Chaste Maid* and *The Maid's Tragedy*] we all benefited greatly from being able to rehearse in the theatre.

Acoustically, the theatre feels very resonant and actors hear their voice coming back to them. It works better when full than when it is empty. It is a space that seems to like people; the audience gives support to the sound, when empty it can echo a little. To be heard better in the space; for the audience to be engaged with what the actor is saying, the actors need to use their training and skills to the full. To give clarity to the word. It isn't a question of volume; constant loudness will lose texture and truth. It's much more a question of how we use the voice in the modern way – we tend to let the sound go away at the end of sentences. In the Globe, actors have to complete the ends of their words and sentences. They also need to use the full range and resonance of the voice and to support it fully with the breath. Light, unsupported voices tend to get lost.

As the actors grew more confident they began to be able to read (or should I say, hear) the space better and to free themselves from any tendency to push the sound out. We're used to spaces where the actor speaks out in a 'V' shape; at the Globe the sound needs to travel in an arc. The openness of the stage and theatre and the lack of set and props means the actors lack the support of resonance around them – it's open on three sides. All this means a different way of working for the actors.

As for the way language worked in the theatre, I think the more actors are encouraged to allow the language to express the emotion, rather than push the feelings into the voice, the better it works. Again, it is a matter of dealing with modern speech habits – you can't speak Shakespearean language on the back foot – you need to have a complete commitment of energy to be able to deliver heightened language. Poetry is a gift to the audience for meaning and sense if it is used fully. Many modern plays deal with sub-texts, but with Shakespeare the word is the characters' thoughts at the moment they speak them. I think the opening season showed us how much is revealed to us by an open, clear delivery of Shakespeare's words (and this was particularly true of the *Henry V*), and much of this clarity was brought out by the actors' awareness of the audience – a fact that is so unavoidable in the shared light of the Globe.

Sue Lefton, Movement Coach: *Henry V, A Chaste Maid, The Winter's Tale, The Maid's Tragedy*
The Globe space heightens the challenges of performing classical plays in large places. In more conventional theatres all of the focus of the audience is on the stage, the lighting, the elaborate set. At the Globe, it's the actor, the text and the audience. The actor's body has more demands made on it; you cannot separate the physical from the text. For an actor it means that your vocal and physical quality is like one mask. You have to give clarity to the movement, to give it shape, colour and plasticity. Everything has to be strongly expressed, so that the audience can feel, 'I don't understand the language, but I do understand what's going on.' The Globe doesn't respond to 'greyness'; it responds to strong definition. Basically it encourages a movement that culminates in a larger physical expression that has to be very clear, that is not always naturalistic, but which is definitely not grand gestures. I think all theatre has an element of satire, a showing up and revealing of the way the world is. It pushes qualities that make the world work the way it does. Theatre is not a literal piece of work; it's about exemplification, stylization; it's not like real life. At the Globe, it's a question of 'How do you present something rhythmically and dynamically?' If the actor is unspecific it shows in an unfocused space, open to the air, without controlled lighting.

Warm-ups before performances are particularly important at the Globe. For the Opening Season our Movement team found that the period of training for the actors paved the way for making movement stronger and at the same time, relaxed. The actors had voice and movement classes every day. The body needs to be more elastic, more expansive on the Globe stage. I think the actors met the challenge very well. They were relaxed, and at the same time energized. When they got on to the stage it was a question of effortlessly filling it, rather than struggling to fill the space with big gestures. They felt exposed in a new way but able to open out and accept the demands on the quality of energy required by the space.

Matthew Scurfield, Actor: Exeter in *Henry V*; Yellowhammer in *A Chaste Maid*; the Duke in *The Two Gentlemen of Verona*
The audience are very aware...they let you know what they're thinking, although they're quite polite – I should think in Elizabethan days audiences were not quite as polite. It's fantastic and nerve-wracking at the same time. I don't think the preparation is any different from playing a conventional theatre. The rehearsal period is more intense, perhaps. You have to penetrate the play more deeply so that we know what we're doing in each moment of the play, so that you're never at a loose end. You have to know what is happening every second when you're on the stage, particularly when you're saying nothing. Even if only two people are watching you, you're very noticeable when you're on this stage. The spontaneity of the audience is wonderful. One can't project what's going to happen. I think a good feeling to have on that stage is of not quite knowing what's going to happen next. There's so much in the regular theatre that helps you to know what can happen next – the lighting, the music. In this theatre, it's vital that actors are *alive* and very much in the present.

I think playing *The Two Gentlemen of Verona* in the Prologue season was probably helpful. I was incredibly nervous the last week of rehearsals on stage for *Two Gentlemen*. It felt like a 'temple' to Shakespeare; you felt overawed. We just wanted to get the play right. For *Henry V* we wore period clothing, but I don't think playing in costume makes much difference to me, to be quite honest. I think initially it does. It's like going out to a party – you're very self-conscious about what you're wearing, but then you forget it. You have the first dress rehearsal, then when you start to play the play clothes become peripheral. As long as you feel comfortable, you kind of forget what you're wearing after a time. I was a little bit nervous at the beginning about the rushes because they were tripping us up but that soon got solved. The acoustics are better than in the Prologue season [when the stage was a temporary structure of plywood and scaffolding]. With *Henry V* I think we just grabbed the stage and embraced what it has to offer, which has a lot to do with Richard [Olivier] and his ritual work. Allowing us to see everyone's pain, grief, insecurity, made us more secure with one another.

For a director it might be easier to have a design, lighting – the whole concept. Here, all you've got is the text and the actor, basically – and the costume. It's mainly text and actors. I think if you're not comfortable with that – going into the actor's imagination and making the text live – then it would be difficult. It's very hard to impose a concept on a play here. That's fine. But here you have to be prepared to almost come in with a blank sheet, sharing with the actors doubts about how the play may or may not work. What seems to be very obscure on the page to many of the actors, becomes clear if the text is approached in this more open way. With *Chaste Maid* I think the Globe revealed this play. You have to be brave enough to let it reveal itself. You see it revealed at the Globe – all the innuendo, the sexual references, what the text means. The building does it. Give the Globe a chance and let it reveal the play rather than thinking we control it. We do to a certain extent.

It's so obvious when you go in there – 1500 people plus the actors, that's it's never going to be one individual that dominates. People have been amazed at the reaction in *Henry*. You have to have the approach open-ended otherwise you won't find out what it's like. You can't put a stamp on it before it's had its time.

For example, soliloquies at the Globe become a very sharing thing, considering that it's very private as well. Although you're talking to 1500 people on your own it feels really private. It feels like you're able to feel really private and secret, and the playgoer feels the actor is talking to him/her as an individual. Having worked here it's so obvious a soliloquy has to be shared with the audience. To let us, as the audience, into the play; to bring us into that situation; to make us more involved. As an actor, you realize you can't deliver soliloquies – for example, Hamlet's 'To be' to yourself. We'll become more adept, better actors at the Globe as the years go on. The communication between the actors and the audience will become more and more personal, a real relationship. Just imagine 'To be or not to be': Hamlet letting us in on his terrible dilemma. I think we mustn't allow ourselves to come to any conclusions about playing the space, and to try to go even further.

Steven Skybell, Actor: Constable of France/Scroop/Bates in *Henry V*; Touchwood Senior in *A Chaste Maid*
One of the amazing surprises of this space is that you'd expect with such an open space, one would have to play broad, with *big* gestures, sweeping movement, but it was such an unexpected delight when I realized that the audience could pick out the movement of an eyebrow. They really could see things; they really are watching, the realization that they could see even small things, that was the real lesson for me. I wouldn't have thought that would be possible, yet it's proved true again and again. The audience are also really *listening*.

You'd think where we are in history – with cameras and film, you would think this space calls for a less subtle form of acting, but in fact you can have trust that a nuance can be read. This space allows for a subtlety you wouldn't expect. To me, I think that one of the most refreshing aspects of this space is that the audience gets totally engaged and verbalizes that engagement. I'm sure in Shakespeare's day actors had to deal with the kind of distraction we sometimes had from the audience. You can't predict 'This is going to be a quiet moment' because if someone shouts something at me, then I have to deal with it.

You have to create a true compelling world on that stage. Everything counts in this theatre. You can't bet on anything. Nothing can be set.

Bill Stewart, Actor: Nym in *Henry V*; Snoop/Mistress Jugg in *A Chaste Maid*
Luckily, we did two different kinds of show – *Henry* which is in the main, straight, and *Chaste Maid* which is a comedy. But they both demanded a certain kind of style because you *can* see the audience in front of you. It's a different style of working than in an ordinary theatre. You have to take the focus yourself, rather than the focus being given by lights. The main thing is you have to be quite open, a more open outgoing style, I think. You needed a lot of energy, the kind of energy is not a tiring energy at all, it's a sort of joyful energy.

I think if the audience is told you can shout or boo and hiss if you want to, you'd expect a lot of it. But there were very few coming ready to do that. Mainly I think they respond in a quite genuine way. Because it's sort of open-air, people feel freer to respond.

I didn't find it at all distracting. I think there was a surprise the first time we got a few rowdies in the audience, but you got used to it very quickly. I still find the pillars a problem. I was very conscious of them at times but I got used to people at the sides of stage quickly – I've worked a lot of the Crucible in Sheffield so I'm used to that kind of space.

When we went on to the stage from the small rehearsal room we did have to readjust things once we were there. When we first came out it was like footballers coming out of a tunnel. You know, you come out, and the crowd are going 'Yeah!' It's not like a pop concert It's like a football stadium.

Ben Walden, Actor: Bardolph/ Montjoy/ Alice in *Henry V* ; Tim in *A Chaste Maid*; Speed in *The Two Gentlemen of Verona*
Playing at the Globe is very, very different because it's much more primal and I suspect much more what theatre was originally intended to be. The actor and the audience is much, much closer. The audience seems much more part of the play. It's different from a vast theatre when they're out there in the darkness and there's a big divide between the actual action of the play and the audience. Here, it's much more give-and-take than in a normal theatre which makes it certainly more exciting for the actor and, judging from when I've watched other plays, more exciting for the audience too. A lot of the reverence that there is in modern theatres goes and it becomes more anarchic.

One of the things you can't do is force people to come and see something they don't want to see. When there were some children who had been forced to come to see the production, when that sort of thing happens, you can feel the audience being negative – you can feel the audience in any theatre but you feel it particularly strongly here. Therefore any distraction – their fidgeting, for example, was very very palpable. But if their fidgeting and lack of attention (because they don't want to be there *at all*) gets to you, you are playing the space incorrectly. It is a *free* space, and the audience can come and go as they wish. You cannot say some reactions are allowed, but not others. Whatever the audience is doing in the yard, you have to get beyond them to all the other people who are behind them in the galleries. This theatre is totally infectious. Everyone's sharing everything.

Preparing a role for this space is not really that different. In the rehearsal room it's virtually identical, but then there's a big big jump when you get on to the stage here. Once you get into this space it's what the Globe stage demands. What it demands of you is that you give everything. There are a lot of acting spaces where what you do can be very delicate, very subtle, and at the Globe you can manage to do that as well, but you have to act at full-beam. It's not really a place where you can hide at all. So what this stage does is it blows you up to maximum energy. Everything that you're doing, every action you make, you play with much more strength. You can play things at a very high level because the stage can take it. If you play things at a low level you have a real problem. The stage responds very well to high energy. And the challenge is to have that energy but to have variations in what you're doing. It loves things being at maximum energy. It's not to do with big gestures. Big gestures are external – that's not so important, it's the inner life that has to be really strong. You can go further and further *and further* and the stage will always embrace it.

Actually you don't notice how big the stage is. One of the things I feel after two summers playing at the Globe, is that I still feel I don't do enough to embrace the very back of the audience – not the Lord's Rooms – but the gentlemen's boxes. They are very easy to forget. You have to remember that they are there all the time. There is a tendency to get in front of the pillars out front but that 'out front' is right the way round behind you, it's a circular space, so there is no 'out front' here and you have to remember to play all the circle – back, sides and front. It's something that's got to be learnt. You have to play the whole stage, not just to the front. You can't just act at one level.

I think that anything that's pre-planned is likely to get shaken around a lot once it's taken on to the stage. Having the experience of doing *The Two Gentlemen of Verona* in the Prologue season didn't really make much difference except that we felt a bit like guinea pigs in a way. All through the rehearsals for *Two Gents* there was a fear of what it would be like to get on to the stage, that big space. The first night was a revelation: it was the best theatre I'd ever played in. When I first went out on to that stage I realized something *really* special had been created in theatre. I was in the first scene of *Two Gents* and I remember opening the door and walking on to the stage and feeling, 'Oh God, this is going to be incredible!' The audience – they went wild that night. Right from the start I thought this is going to change theatre, change the way people do theatre. And I think in the long term it will. It will take a long time but I think anyone who works here will never quite see acting in the same way again, because of the energy created and because it makes it clear what theatre is really about. It's for people to meditate on their condition. It really makes that clear in a way that is almost indescribable. And the energy it gives you and the enthusiasm for playing it gives you I don't think ever leaves you after you've done it. So the revelation on that first night of that Prologue season year was realizing that this is an incredible new theatre that actors all over the world will long to play in, and I'm here right at the start. I felt very lucky. For the following year, I was relieved that I didn't have the fear of what it would be like working in that theatre because I'd done it before but the fact that it's a different production, a different rehearsal process, seems like a totally different job but the magic that is in that theatre is basically the same.

I think the role of director is different in this theatre and I think that for directors a very strict directorial vision of how a play should look will get broken up here, because the play gets pulled around by the audience shouting out, bawling and all that. Nothing is bigger than the energy that happens once the audience are there, and so anything that's pre-planned is likely to get shaken around a lot. But the play *must* hold its shape. If the audience are allowed to take over it can get sloppy and self-indulgent.

It's a wonderful storytelling place. It's very easy to listen here. When I saw *The Maid's Tragedy* last night – I've never read and never seen a production of it – I found it very easy to understand. I'm sure that was partly because the performances were good, but it's very clear, you can hear very well, the story is made very clear. It is a wonderful listening space. The clarity of what you're saying is so much easier. It's much easier to understand Shakespeare in this theatre, I think.

Vincent Brimble, Actor: Gower/Mistress Quickly in *Henry V*; Sixpence/ Mistress Fork in *A Chaste Maid*
The closest to it is the open-air work I've done. You have to play large and broad, but the major aspect that makes this so different from anywhere else is the way the audience is involved, and without any particular prompting from us, they seem to expect to be involved, to become involved in a way that doesn't really happen anywhere else, which becomes ultimately a part of the performance.

And that gives an energy you need, it feeds into the play, feeds into the actor but also feeds back into the audience, especially to the seated people who pick up the energy from the groundlings and ultimately come down and join them. That happened quite a lot. Quite a few people would come out of the galleries and down to the yard because it just looked like the place to be. I think it is the best place to watch the show. It's hard work being a groundling; quite tiring. Also it's not easy when it's fairly crowded to find a place where you can see easily. I have to say the pillars create problems. Obviously they have qualities, and add a great quality to the look of the place. I think it seems when the Globe was rebuilt it's quite possible that they didn't have pillars at all, that they spanned right across the stage with a double gable, and I think it's possible that they did that because they felt it was an advantage to do it and I can just imagine watching a performance with no pillars from any position in that wonderful space would be amazing. They obviously have a certain function – you can play about them, around them, but they do create enormous sightline problems. It's not that you feel trapped by them but the problem with the pillars is they do tend to pull you down to the front. It makes it feel like a proscenium stage. The light gets very dingy at the back of the stage in the afternoon. Shakespeare's company, we know, were interested in playing indoor theatres.

You to have maintain a certain flexibility, a sensitivity to the way the audience is receiving things; whether you pump things up; whether you hold things down, whether you increase your volume especially when planes are likely to fly over at any moment.

But you have to keep things very loosely blocked so you can move around, that's always true in the round anyway – that you should never stay in one place too long if you possibly can. You tend to work on diagonals, but especially if you're going to have a large obstruction in the way that you also get in the galleries where there are wooden pillars. When you have set scenes – as in *Chaste Maid*, where you have a long scene set around a bed, for instance, you can't do anything about that but it does mean you have a whole scene where some people have a very poor view, or no view at all in some cases. If you don't see people it's often hard to hear them. Comedy is always difficult to play in the round anyway because it has to be very big, but also because if you raise one eyebrow in the round or on three sides – half the audience are going to be able to see it, the other half aren't. There are attendant difficulties, but comedy certainly works amazingly well on this stage. You don't know what's going to happen when you go on to the stage. The audience throws everything at you – literally.

Christian Camargo, Actor: Dauphin/Isabel/Grey in *Henry V*; Touchwood Junior in *A Chaste Maid*

I came as a visitor in the Prologue season to watch. I couldn't get over the architecture of the space, and the beauty of it. Then when I came for the Opening season to actually play the space, I felt awe – as though I were in a high temple, like the chosen playing in this place. It's like being in a church but it's a solemnity that gets cracked by the performance. I was rehearsing at the National Theatre when I came to a performance of *The Two Gentlemen of Verona*. To go from that to this, on a warm sunny day outside, you just came in expecting to enjoy yourself. Whereas you walk in to the National, and you sit and say 'Show me', 'Entertain me'.

I had no expectations of playing this space. It was strange to start rehearsals and see the stage still being made; it put a real freshness to it, and a newness about it. I mean it hasn't been done in how many hundreds of years? So there are no levels to raise to or sink below and you're not competing with the beautiful structure either, which is strange. When I first got here as a tourist, I thought how could you compete with this beautiful space as a player doing it for real, but I found as a player there is no sense of competition. It all works together. As a church does, it doesn't exist without the people and without the players. I feel that very strongly as an actor coming into that space and doing a play. There are no expectations and I felt so free and unnervous. Even with all the history attached to it, the history of the Globe and England and English acting, there is such freedom. It's been so calm and a lot of it has to do with Mark [Rylance]. But a lot of it also is the space. It breathes appreciation from all sides.

It's a space that invites everything. I think that everything should be tried in that space. What I've found acting in it and from working with directors is that the space tells you where to go, what to do, how to walk. The space tells you where you need to emphasize this or that, and where you need to be in the space.

Coming from New York where you have conceptual directors who want to tell you where to go, they're the ones that want to have control. This space, because of the way the pillars are, because of the way the stage is set, because the audience is all around you, there's no way for you to have control over your movements without respecting the stage itself, without listening to it.

When you're preparing a play, in the rehearsal rooms you set; you have to set what you want, of course, but you have to be willing to give up on that when you get into the space. You have to be willing to respect the stage.

Malcolm McKay, Director: *A Chaste Maid in Cheapside*
I love the space. What makes it different from other theatres is that you have 500 people standing. The excitement generated by that mobility makes everything much more fluid. If I was to design a theatre now I would use that kind of space as a model. I would bring lights in, and probably get rid of the pillars, or have the choice of using pillars or not. It is a great space. Everything is very much an experiment at the moment, and there's something of a museum piece about it, but I think once the newness is gone, it'll be better. I'll be very interested to see the big tragedies in this space. I don't think I approached the text any differently. I felt my purpose was to take that text and make it incredibly clear to the audience. I think *Richard III* would be terrific here.

Jack Shepherd, Director: *The Two Gentlemen of Verona*
I was surprised at how big the theatre was when I first saw it. I could see the whole space working wonderfully well. My only anxieties were ... the stageposts, the audibility of the actors. I don't think you have to approach the space differently. But volume, diction, clarity of thought, attention to metre, etc. are much more important than in indoor theatres. Any line that is muttered disappears. The key is to keep the language alive without allowing it to be declamatory.

There are two areas of poor visibility brought about by the position and thickness of the pillars. The atmosphere generated by actors and audience was very powerful. The sharing of the play was more intense than is usual. Although the comments made by the audience were very self-conscious, often embarrassingly so. At least they were *contributing*, or trying to. On a good night the 'collective unconscious' was at work. The only production I've been in before which had a similar 'shared experience' was *The Mysteries* at the National Theatre. The columns are very useful, providing walkways for the actors, and enabling people to hide behind them.

Gaynor MacFarlane, Director: *Damon and Pythias*

I suppose that, like many others, I was surprised by how big the Globe seemed at first sight. We have been conditioned by C. Walter Hodges *et al.* and by the relatively modest scale of the Rose excavations to expect the Globe to be a small and intimate theatre. In reality, it has an 'epic' quality to it, the echo of Greek and Roman amphitheatres. Of course this sense of scale is most striking when the theatre is empty. Importantly, it is the audience, the faces and bodies of spectators, which create the sense of intimacy so crucial to performance in the Globe. The theatre is a remarkably different place when one is standing on the stage and when one is in the auditorium. From the stage it is warmer and more intimate, smaller, even.

The theatre also seemed new, a fact that I emphasised with the company as much as possible: there are no ghosts, we are not steeped in history. What I was concerned with was making a lively, vital, immediate production for a 1996 audience, and with solving as many of the 'problems' and challenges of the space in the limited time. I think that the premise that this is a space that is difficult to play is erroneous. It simply demands a different kind of approach to the playing space. However, this is true of all theatres that a director works in inasmuch as it would be wrong-headed to approach the Olivier space in the same way as one would approach a small space like the Gate. At first the stage struck me as vast (perhaps as a result of having worked mainly in small studio venues) but not unwieldy. *It never occurred to me* that the pillars would be a handicap but that they might offer interesting opportunities for actors to create and define a particular acting space, and to hide, eavesdrop or just lean. The positioning of the pillars was helpful in providing an entrance or exit to the side-doors, an idea of journeying or a place from which to share confidences with the audience. The auditorium clearly worked best when absolutely packed with people. It struck me that the least successful seating and therefore the least interesting place to be seated was on the banked benches around the yard. Clearly the view from the galleries is largely unobstructed and the picture or 'dance' of the play is thrown into relief from those vantage-points. The experience of being a groundling is the most interactive and therefore, I suspect, the most rewarding for an audience-member. To play successfully to all of these areas, the actors have to be resourceful, open and extraordinarily adaptive.

The only difference from other spaces in terms of the rehearsal process is the absolute necessity of keeping the scale, physical dimensions and open roof of the Globe in mind at all times. Emotionally and in terms of energy, psychology and motivation, the process is as detailed and rigorous as possible. The *Damon and Pythias* company was fortunate in having Mondays to rehearse in the theatre which made an enormous difference. We were able to play in the theatre, talking to each other from various galleries and boxes, singing, calling and generally acclimatizing to the scale and demands of the theatre. We also played on stage, exploring the best positions for asides, for dominating the stage, for scenes with one or many actors and with getting on and off stage into the 'press' (groundlings). I also found it important to move around the theatre all the time to watch and hear the actors on stage. I can only comment that I cannot imagine that a director can create a successful show in the Globe without being extremely mobile throughout the auditorium during rehearsals on stage.

Rebecca Lenkiewicz, Actor: Outlaw/stage hand/Prostitute, *The Two Gentlemen of Verona*
My first reaction? Absolutely beautiful – it was very enclosed and like a world in itself. It felt quite intimate as a space. The stage seemed much much bigger than the rehearsal space despite accurate mark-ups. The first run-through felt as if one would topple off the stage – it wasn't a nice space to play without the audience – a bit jagged, with no real 'focus' of the usual proscenium arch. Once full, the experience was transformed and it felt as though the stage and house itself were completely filled with the actions of the actors – brilliant when it was full. It's completely different from other theatre spaces. The seated audiences were similar to other audiences but the groundlings were completely transformed. The freedom of standing and the communal nature of it produced more reaction and warmth and participation.

I saw both *A Midsummer* and *Damon* and was enchanted by being a groundling though I was not quite taken away by sitting down. Standing was far better and I was amazed at the details that can be seen – it feels as if one could 'wing' certain movements on stage but nothing goes by unnoticed. I think the whole place is far more sensitive to audience energy than any other theatre could possibly be.

Maureen Beattie, Actor: *Damon and Pythias*
I was very moved and excited and immediately put in a wish to the great producer in the sky that I might one day get a chance to work in the Globe. We had the advantage of seeing two productions, *Two Gents* and *Dream* in the theatre, and of rehearsing in the theatre on Mondays. The Globe is utterly unlike any other space I've worked and I would say it's essential to get as much time on the actual stage as possible. Our production was performed for the public only once. It was strangely undaunting, very friendly. The expectation was that the audience were going to enjoy themselves. There was a feeling that the audience were a real part of the proceedings. I was aware more than ever before that the audience is made up of individuals rather than just being a mass of humanity, and yet they were also an entity, a single entity. Most obviously, of course, the audience actually vocalized their responses – which was great fun for us.

I think the Globe demands, vocally, the old art of *projection* – the ability to send the words and emotions out to the audience without shouting or losing subtlety. Also, physically the actor has to be very *definite* about moves and gestures – anything 'woolly' just doesn't read somehow. This may have something to do with the lack of defining light on the acting space. The actor also has to be aware of the audience being almost all around her/him – upwards as well! And yet, you can turn your back on the bulk of the audience and still be in 'focus'.

The only un-focused area of the stage *I* felt was the balcony, which seems to withdraw backwards out of the performing area. I would like to see the balcony perhaps brought forward to overhang the main acting area. I know there has been much talk about whether or not the actors should make use of the auditorium as an extension of the acting area. I don't know what happened at the real Globe but I am convinced that it works wonderfully and helps that feeling that the audience and the actors are all in it together. I think our particular case is interesting in that we were only ever going to perform *Damon* once and that fed into the feel of immediacy you get at the Globe.

Appendix: New Globe Acting Companies, 1996–97

Prologue Season, 1996

The Two Gentlemen of Verona

Valentine	Lennie James
Proteus	Mark Rylance
Silvia	Anastasia Hille
Julia	Stephanie Roth
Duke	Matthew Scurfield
Launce	Jim Bywater
Speed	Ben Walden
Lucetta	Aicha Kossoko
Panthino/Eglamour	Graham Brown
Antonio/Thurio	George Innes
Host/stand-in Thurio	Steven Alvey
Attendants	Rebecca Lenkiewicz
	Andrew Fielding
Director	Jack Shepherd
Music by	Claire van Kampen

Opening Season, 1997

The Life of Henry the Fifth

King of France/Bishop of Ely/Erpingham	William Russell
Isabel/The Dauphin/Grey	Christian Camargo
Princess Katherine/ the Boy	Toby Cockerell
Constable of France/Scroop/Bates	Steven Skybell
Orleans/Burgundy/Williams	Rory Edwards
Rambures/Cambridge/MacMorris	Craig Pinder
Montjoy/Alice/Bardolph	Ben Walden
Governor of Harfleur/Pistol/Canterbury	John McEnery
King Henry	Mark Rylance
Gloucester	David Lear
Bedford/Jamy	Nick Fletcher
Westmorland/Nym	Bill Stewart
Exeter	Matthew Scurfield
Llwellyn	David Fielder

Gower/Mistress Quickly   Vincent Brimble

Director   Richard Olivier
Designer   Jenny Tiramani
Musical Director   Phillip Pickett

The Winter's Tale
Hermione   Belinda Davison
Leontes   Mark Lewis-Jones
Perdita/Mamillius   Anna-Livia Ryan
Paulina   Joy Richardson
Camillo   Ade Sapara
Antigonus/3rd Gentleman   Andrew Bridgmont
Cleomenes   Chris Porter
Dion   Mike Dowling
Emilia   Lucy Campbell
Polixenes   Michael Gould
Florizel   Jonathan Slinger
Old Shepherd   Patrick Godfrey
Clown   Dean Atkinson
Autolycus   Nicholas Le Prevost
First Lady   Polly Pritchett

Director   David Freeman
Designer   Tom Phillips
Composer   Claire van Kampen
Costume Supervisor   Susan Coates

A Chaste Maid in Cheapside
Yellowhammer   Matthew Scurfield
Maudlin   Amelda Brown
Tim   Ben Walden
Moll   Katie MacNichol
Tutor   William Russell
Sir Walter Whorehound   Rory Edwards
Sir Oliver Kix/Mistress Tool   John McEnery
Lady Kix   Eve Matheson
Allwit   Mark Rylance
Mistress Allwit   Elizabeth Meadows Rouse
Welshwoman/Sir Walter's Whore/   Jules Melvin
    Mistress Underman
Davy   David Fielder
Touchwood Senior   Steven Skybell
Touchwood Junior   Christian Camargo
Sixpence/Mistress Fork   Vincent Brimble

Snoop/Mistress Jugg	Bill Stewart
Sims/Mistress Bun	Nick Fletcher
Stephen/Mistress Book	Toby Cockerell
Dick/Nurse/Waterman	David Lear
Robert/Parson/Waterman	Craig Pinder
Director	Malcolm McKay
Designer	Jenny Tiramani
Composer and Musical Director	Claire van Kampen

The Maid's Tragedy

King	Nicholas Le Prevost
Amintor	Jonathan Slinger
Evadne	Geraldine Alexander
Lysippus	Andrew Bridgmont
Melantius	Mark Lewis-Jones
Diphilus	Michael Gould
Aspatia	Anna-Livia Ryan
Calianax	Patrick Godfrey
Cleon	Dean Atkinson
Strato	Jonathan Bond
Antiphilia/Sea Monster	Lucy Campbell
Dula/Night	Joy Richardson
Lady in waiting/Cynthia	Belinda Davison
Gentleman of the Bedchamber/Neptune	Mike Dowling
Diagoras	Chris Porter
Director	Lucy Bailey
Designer	Angela Davies
Composer	Jane Gardner

Notes

1 Introduction

1. Pauline Kiernan, 'Findings from the Globe Workshop Season 1995', http://www.rdg.ac.uk/globe/Data-Base/Articles/Workshop.html

2. The Space of the Audience

1. J. L. Styan, *Shakespeare's Stagecraft* (Cambridge, 1967), p. 230.
2. Attributed to Webster in E.K. Chambers, *The Elizabethan Stage* (4 vols, Oxford, 1923), IV, pp. 257–8; hereinafter cited as *ES*.
3. For quotations from Jonson's plays see *Works*, ed. C. H. Herford, and Percy and Evelyn M. Simpson, 11 vols (Oxford, 1954).
4. Robin May (ed.), *The Wit of the Theatre* (London, 1969), p. 7. The gap that divided audience and actors at the Stratford Memorial Theatre, known in the business as the 'great chasm', was not finally rectified until the 1960s.
5. Thomas Middleton and Thomas Dekker, *The Roaring Girl*, ed. Elizabeth Cook; New Mermaids (2nd edn, London, 1997). Cook notes that in the 1983 Royal Shakespeare Company production of the play the actor scanned the audience as he spoke these lines, 'making the auditorium of the Shakespeare Memorial Theatre the galleries of Sir Alexander's overcrowded house' (p. xxiii).
6. John Weever, *The Mirror of Martyrs* (London, 1601), A3v, F3v
7. Francis Bacon, *The Advancement of Learning*, Bk II, Ch. 13.
8. Thomas Nashe, *Pierce Penniless his Supplication to the Devil* in *Works*, ed. R.B. McKerrow (Oxford, 1957; rev. F. P. Wilson, 1966), I, 212.
9. Phillip Stubbes, *The Anatomie of Abuses*, ed. F. J. Furnivall (London: New Shakespeare Society, 1877–79)
10. Quoted in *ES*, I.265n.
11. See Martha Tuck Rozett, *The Doctrine of Election and the Emergence of Elizabethan Tragedy* (Princeton, NJ, 1984), pp. 19–20.
12. For the Florentine Antimo Galli's account of the Venetian ambassador's visit to the Curtain in 1613, see Andrew Gurr, *Playgoing in Shakespeare's London* (Cambridge, 1987), pp. 71; 227.
13. *Calendar of State Papers Venetian 1617–19*, pp. 67–8; quoted in Gurr, *The Shakespearean Stage* (Cambridge, 1972), p. 217.
14. John Webster, 'To the Reader', *The White Devil*, ed. John Russell Brown (London, 1960).
15. Middleton(?) *Father Hubburd's Tale* (1604), B4r, CIV DIr.
16. Thomas Dekker, *The Non-Dramatic Works*, ed. A. B. Gosart, 5 vols (London, 1884–6), II.92.
17. Penguin Classics (Harmondsworth, 1985), pp. 273–5.

18. Styan, p. 228.
19. For a discussion of the treatment of mimetic illusion in the play-within-the play in *Love's Labour's Lost* and *A Midsummer Night's Dream*, see Pauline Kiernan, *Shakespeare's Theory of Drama* (Cambridge, 1986), pp. 100–16.
20. All play references are to the Oxford *Complete Works*, eds Stanley Wells and Gary Taylor (Oxford, 1986), unless otherwise stated.
21. On the reconstruction and design of the new Globe, see the chapters by John Orrell, Andrew Gurr and Jon Greenfield in J.R. Mulryne and Margaret Shewring (eds), *Shakespeare's Globe Rebuilt* (Cambridge 1997).
22. Michael Goldman, *Shakespeare and the Energies of Drama* (Princeton, 1972), p. 4.
23. William Davenant, Epilogue, *News from Plymouth* (1635).
24. *The Independent*, 23 August 1996.
25. Maurice Evans (ed.) *Elizabethan Sonnets* (London, 1977), p. 107.
26. Styan, pp. 75–6.
27. David Mann, *The Elizabethan Player: Contemporary Stage Representation* (London, 1991), pp. 210–11.
28. Just before this passage, there is the more famous allusion to the boy companies of the indoor theatres taking away custom from the public theatres:

> *Rosencrantz*. . . . there is, sir, an eyrie of children, little eyases, that cry out on the top of question and are most tyrannically clapped fo't. These are now the fashion, and so berattle the common stages – so they call them – that many wearing rapiers are afraid of goose-quills, and dare scarce come thither. (339–44)

29. I have discussed this topic in Kiernan, *Shakespeare's Theory*, passim.
30. 'To the Reader', op. cit. Jonson developed audience abuse into a fine art, of course, in his scripted inductions and prologues; Hamlet is made to voice resentment of actors who indulge in by-play with the audience and thereby disrupt the story: 'And let those that play your clowns speak no more than is set down for them; for there be of them that will themselves laugh, to set on some quantity of barren spectators to laugh too, though in the mean time some necessary question of the play then to be considered' (3.2.38–43).
31. Leonard Digges wrote of playgoers at performances of *Julius Caesar*, 'Oh how the Audience/Were ravish'd, with what wonder they went thence…' (Commendatory Verses to Shakespeare's Poems, 1604), quoted in *WS* II, p. 233.
32. Thomas Dekker, *The Gull's Hornbook*, Chapter 6.
33. '…you think you have undone me, think so still, and swallow that belief, till you be company for court-hand clerks, and starved Attournies, till you break in at plays like prentices for three a groat, and crack nuts with the scholars in penny rooms again, and fight for Apples, till you return to what I found you…'. Fletcher, *Wit Without Money*, 1614, IV.i.

34 Quoted in Gurr, *Playgoing*, p. 230.
35 John Stephens, *Satirical Characters and Others*, p. 292 (V4v), quoted in Gurr, *Playgoing*, p. 228.
36 *Observer*, 25 August 1996.

3. Dramatic Illusion in the Open Playhouse

1. Michael Goldman, *Shakespeare and the Energies of Drama* (Princeton, NJ., 1972) p. 6.
2. Thomas Kyd, *The Spanish Tragedy*, ed. R. J. Mulryne (London, 1989).
3. Cyril Tourneur, *The Atheist's Tragedy*, in *Jacobean Tragedies*, ed. A.H. Gomme (Oxford, 1969), pp. 227–35.
4. I have silently replaced the Oxford editors' 'Sir John' with the more familiar name 'Falstaff'. This scene is discussed along with other scenes in Shakespeare which focus on dramatic illusion in Kiernan, *Shakespeare's Theory*, pp. 91–126.
5. Quoted in Gurr, *Playgoing*, p. 126.
6. 'See T. M. Raysor (ed.) *Coleridge's Shakespearean Criticism*, 2 vols, London, 1930), I, pp. 129, 200, 202. 'Willing suspension of disbelief' is from *Biographia Literaria* (ch. 14) ed. John Shawcross, 2 vols (Oxford, 1907), 274–5.
7. Samuel Johnson, *Selected Writings*, ed. Patrick Cruttwell (Harmondsworth, 1968; repr. 1982), pp. 274–5; 296–7. Johnson's writings on Shakespeare have been frequently misinterpreted. In his notes to the plays and his *Prefaces to Shakespeare* he shows a strong awareness of the playwright as a working professional producing plays for performance: 'let it be remembered that our author well knew what would please the audience for which he wrote' (p. 296).
8. Quoted in *WS*, pp. 233–4.
9. *WS*, p. 232.
10. See Kiernan, *Shakespeare's Theory*, passim.
11. Stephens, *Satyrical Essayes*, p. 297 (V7r), quoted in Gurr, *Playgoing*, p. 228.
12. Quoted in Gamini Salgado (ed.), *Eyewitnesses of Shakespeare* (Sussex, 1975), pp. 37–8.
13. Quoted in Salgado, pp. 38–9.
14. Thomas Nashe, *Pierce Penniless his Supplication to the Devil*, in *Works*, ed. R. B. McKerrow, reprinted with corrections and notes by F. P. Wilson (Oxford, 1966), I, 212.
15. *The Christmas Prince*, ed. F. S. Boas and W. W. Greg (Malone Society, Oxford, 1923).
16. William E. Gruber: 'The Actor in the Script: Affective Strategies in Shakespeare's *Antony and Cleopatra*'. *Comparative Drama*, 19 (Spring 1985) 30–48.
17. Michael Goldman, *Shakespeare and the Energies of Drama*, p. 6.
18. Recent studies include Stephen Orgel, *Impersonations: the Performance of Gender in Shakespeare's England* (Cambridge, 1996); Michael Shapiro, *Gender in Play on the Shakespearean Stage:*

Boy Heroines and Female Pages (Ann Arbor, 1994); Marjorie Garber, *Vested Interests: Cross-Dressing and Cultural Anxiety* (London, 1991).

19. Bruce R. Smith, *Homosexual Desire in Shakespear's England* (Chicago and London, 1991), p. 150.
20. Lady Mary Wroth, in her prose romance *Urania* compares real women with women as played by boys on the stage when she describes a man's response to one of her heroines showing that he 'was no further wrought than if he had seen a delicate play-boy act a loving woman's part, and knowing him a boy, like only his action'. See Michael Shapiro, 'Lady Wroth Describes a "Boy Actress"', *Medieval and Renaissance Drama in England*, 4, ed. J. Leeds Barroll (New York, 1987), pp. 187–94, where the quotation is discussed.
21. Part of the process of cutting the play involved removing characters from certain scenes, and the Dauphin was drafted into scenes where he does not appear in Shakespeare's play. For the details of the cuts and changes to the text, see Part II.
22. David Mann, *The Elizabethan Player*, p. 26.

4 Dramaturgy, 3-D Staging and Daylight Space

1. Styan, p. 81.
2. For this translation from the original German, see David Klein, 'Did Shakespeare Produce His Own Plays?', *Modern Language Review* 57 (1962), 556–60.
3. James L. Calderwood, *To Be and Not To Be: Negation and Metadrama in 'Hamlet'* (New York and London, 1983), pp. 167, 167.
4. Dessen, *Recovering*, passim.
5. David Carnegie, 'Stabbed Through the Arras: the Dramaturgy of Elizabethan Stage Hangings' in Heather Kerr, Robin Eden, Madge Mitton (eds), *Shakespeare: World Views* (Delaware, 1996), p. 191. Carnegie offers detailed suggestions for the use of the hangings for the discovery of Hermione.
6. For examples of 'early entrances' and the symbolic use of stage doors, see Alan C. Dessen's stimulating study of Elizabethan staging practices, *Rediscovering Shakespeare's Theatrical Vocabulary* (Cambridge, 1995).
7. Mariko Ichikawa, 'Exits in Shakespeare's Plays: Time Allowed to Exiters', *Studies in English Literature*, 68 (Tokyo, 1992), 189–206.
8. It would be instructive to experiment with Andrew Gurr's suggestion for staging the chair of state in *Hamlet* in the *locus* or 'authority' position so that Claudius is facing the *frons*. See Gurr, 'The Bare Island', *Shakespeare Survey* 47 (1994), 39.
9. See Siobhan Keenan and Peter Davidson, 'The Iconography of the Bankside Globe' and John Ronayne, '*Totus Mundus Agit Histrionem*: the Interior Decoration Scheme of the Bankside Globe', R. Mulryne and Margaret Shewring (eds), both in *Shakespeare's Globe Rebuilt* (Cambridge, 1997), pp. 121–46; and 147–54.
10. Styan, p. 172.

5 Preparing the Play for the Globe Space

1. *King Henry V*, ed. Andrew Gurr (Cambridge, 1992). All references to *Henry V* are to this edition unless otherwise stated.
2. 'On the 21st of September, after dinner, at about two o'clock, I and my party went across the water; in the straw thatched house we saw the tragedy of the first Emperor Julius Caesar, very pleasantly performed, with approximately fifteen characters.' Quoted from Ernest Schanzer's translation in his article 'Thomas Platter's Observations on the Elizabethan Stage,' *Notes and Queries*, 201 (1956), 465–7. Thomas Platter visited London from 18 September to 20 October 1599. The Globe was built in 1599.
3. Thomas Platter devoted a great deal of attention to the jig that was performed after the *Julius Caesar* performance he described. 'At the end of the play they danced together admirably and exceedingly gracefully, according to their custom two in each group dressed in men's and two in women's apparel.' Later in the passage is a description of a visit to a theatre at Bishopsgate (almost certainly the Curtain) where 'in conclusion they danced, too, very gracefully, in the English and the Irish mode'. See Schanzer, *Notes & Queries* 201 (1956) 466.

8 Revelations and Discoveries

1. Peter Brook, *The Empty Space* (Harmondsworth, 1982; first published 1968), pp. 89–90.
2. Salic Law denied succession through the female line. If Elizabeth married a French prince there was a danger that England would be ruled by France.

Bibliography

Bacon, Francis, *The Advancement of Learning*, London, 1605.

Barroll, J. Leeds, Alexander Leggatt, Richard Hosley and Alvin Kernan, eds, *The Revels History of Drama in English*, Vol. III, 1576–1613. London, 1975.

Beckerman, Bernard, *Shakespeare and the Globe*, New York, 1962.

——, 'Theatrical Plots and Elizabethan Stage Practice', in *Shakespeare and Dramatic Tradition: Essays in Honor of S. F. Johnson*, ed. W. R. Elton and William B. Long. Newark, 1989, pp. 109–24.

Beaumont, Francis, *The Burning Pestle*, ed. Michael Hattaway, London, 1969.

——, with John Fletcher, *The Maid's Tragedy*, ed. T. W. Craik, Manchester, 1988.

Bentley, G. E., *The Jacobean and Caroline Stage*, 7 vols, Oxford, 1941–68.

——, *The Profession of Dramatist in Shakespeare's Time, 1590–1642*, Princeton, 1971.

——, *The Profession of Player in Shakespeare's Time, 1590–1642*, Princeton, 1984.

Berry, Herbert, *Shakespeare's Playhouses*, New York, 1987.

——, *The First Public Playhouse: the Theatre in Shoreditch, 1576–1598*, Montreal, 1979.

Bethell, S. L., *Shakespeare and the Popular Dramatic Tradition*, London, 1944.

Bevington, David, *From 'Mankind' to Marlowe: Growth and Structure in the Popular Drama of Tudor England*, Cambridge, Mass., 1962.

——, *Tudor Drama and Politics*, Cambridge, Mass., 1968.

Blatherwick, Simon. 'The Archaeological Evaluation of the Globe Playhouse', in *Shakespeare's Globe Rebuilt*, ed. J. R. Mulryne and Margaret Shewring, Cambridge, 1997.

——, (with Andrew Gurr) 'Shakespeare's Factory: Archaeological Evaluation of the Site of the Globe Theatre at 1/15 Anchor Terrace, Southwark Bridge Road, Southwark', *Antiquity* 66 (1992) 315–33.

Booth, Stephen, 'Speculations on Doubling in Shakespeare's Plays' in Philip McGuire and D. Samuelson, eds, *Shakespeare: the Theatre Dimension*, London, 1979.

Bradbrook, Muriel, *Elizabethan Staging Conditions*, Cambridge, 1962.

——, *Themes and Conventions of Elizabethan Tragedy*, Cambridge, 1936.

——, *The Rise of the Common Player*, London, 1962.

——, *Shakespeare the Craftsman: the Clark Lecture for 1968*, London, 1969.

——, *English Dramatic Form*, London, 1965.

——, *The Living Monument*, London, 1976.

——, *The Collected Papers*, 4 vols, Brighton, Sussex, 1982–89.

Bradley, David, *From Text to Performance in the Elizabethan Theatre: Preparing the Play for the Stage*, Cambridge, 1992.

Peter Brook, *The Empty Space*, Harmondsworth, 1982; first published London, 1968.

Brown, John Russell, 'Research in the Service of the Theatre: the Example of Shakespeare Studies', *Theatre Research International*, 18, 25–35.

Calderwood, James L, *To Be and Not To Be: Negation and Metadrama in 'Hamlet'*, New York, 1983.

Carnegie, David, 'Stabbed Through the Arras: the Dramaturgy of Elizabethan Stage Hangings', in *Shakespeare: World Views*, ed. Heather Kerr, Robin Eden, Madge Mitton, Delaware 1996.

Cerasano, S. P., 'Raising a Playhouse from the Dust', *Shakespeare Quarterly* 40 (1989) 483–490.

Chambers, E. K., *The Elizabethan Stage*, 4 vols, Oxford, 1923.

——, *William Shakespeare: a Study of Facts and Problems*, 2 vols, Oxford, 1930.

Coleridge, S. T., *Coleridge's Shakespearean Criticism*, 2 vols, ed. T. M. Raysor, London, 1930.

——, *Collected Letters of Samuel Taylor Coleridge*, 6 vols, ed. Earl Leslie Griggs, Oxford, 1956–71.

Cook, Ann Jennalie, *The Privileged Playgoers of Shakespeare's London, 1576–1642*, Princeton, 1981.

Coveney, Michael, 'Shakespeare Inc.', *The Observer*, 25 August 1996.

Daniel, Samuel, *The Complete Works in Verse and Prose*, ed. A. B. Grosart, 5 vols, London, 1885–96.

Davenant, William, *News from Plymouth*, London, 1635.

Dekker, Thomas, *The Non-Dramatic Works*, ed. A. B. Grosart. 5 vols, London, 1884–86.

Dessen, Alan C., *Elizabethan Stage Conventions and Modern Interpreters*, Cambridge, 1984.

——, *Recovering Shakespeare's Theatrical Vocabulary*, Cambridge, 1995.

——, *Elizabethan Drama and the Viewer's Eye*, Chapel Hill, 1977.

Drayton, Michael, *Idea* sonnet sequence in *Elizabethan Sonnets*, ed. Maurice Evans, London, 1977.

Dutton, Richard, '*Hamlet, An Apology for Actors*, and the Sign of the Globe', *Shakespeare Survey* 41 (1981), 35–42.

Edmond, Mary. 'Peter Street, 1553–1609: Builder of Playhouses', *Shakespeare Survey* 45 (1992), 101–14.

Evans, Maurice, ed. *Elizabethan Sonnets*, London, 1977.

Foakes, R. A., *Illustrations of the English Stage, 1580–1642*, London, 1985.

——, (with) R. T. Tickers, eds, *Henslowe's Diary*, Cambridge, 1961.

Garber, Marjorie, *Vested Interests: Cross-Dressing and Cultural Anxiety*, London, 1991.

Gayton, Edmund, *Pleasant Notes on Don Quixot*, London, 1654.

Graves, R. B., '*The Duchess of Malfi* at the Globe and Blackfriars', *Renaissance Drama*, n.s.9 (1978), 193–209.

Greg, W. W., ed., *Dramatic Documents from the Elizabethan Playhouses*, 2 vols, Oxford, 1931.

Greenfield, Jon, 'Design as Reconstruction/Reconstruction as Design', in *Shakespeare's Globe Rebuilt*, ed. J. R. Mulryne and Margaret Shewring, Cambridge, 1997.

——, 'Timber Framing, the Two Bays and After', in *Shakespeare's Globe Rebuilt*, ed. J. R. Mulryne and Margaret Shewring, Cambridge, 1997.

Goldman, Michael, *Shakespeare and the Energies of Drama*, Princeton, 1972.

Gosson, Stephen, *Plays Confuted in Five Actions*, London, 1582.

——, *The School of Abuse*, London, 1599.

Gruber, William E, 'The Actor in the Script: Affective Strategies in Shakespeare's *Antony and Cleopatra*', *Comparative Drama*, 19 (Spring 1985) 30–48.

Gurr, Andrew, 'Shakespeare's Globe: a History of Reconstruction and Some Reasons for Trying', in *Shakespeare's Globe Rebuilt*, ed. J. R. Mulryne and Margaret Shewring, Cambridge, 1997.

——, 'Staging at the Globe', in *Shakespeare's Globe Rebuilt*, ed. J. R. Mulryne and Margaret Shewring, Cambridge, 1997.

——, *The Shakespearian Playing Companies*, Oxford, 1996.

——, *The Shakespearean Stage*, 3rd edn, Cambridge, 1992.

——, *Playgoing in Shakespeare's London*, 2nd edn, Cambridge, 1997.

—— ed., *King Henry V*, Cambridge, 1992.

——, 'Money or Audiences: the Impact of Shakespeare's Globe', *Theatre Notebook* 42 (1988), 3–14.

——, 'Hearers and Beholders in Shakespearean Drama', *Essays in Theatre*, Vol. 3, no. 1 (Nov. 1984), 30–45.

——, 'A First Doorway into the Globe', *Shakespeare Quarterly* 41 (1990), 97–100.

——, 'The "State" of Shakespeare's Audiences', in *Shakespeare and the Sense of Performance*, ed. Marvin and Ruth Thompson, Newark, 1989, 162–80.

——, 'The Bare Island', *Shakespeare Survey* 47 (1994) 29–43.

——, 'Shakespeare and the Visual Signifier', *Reclamations of Shakespeare*, ed. A. J. Hoenselaars, *Studies in Literature* 15, Amsterdam, Atlanta, GA, 1994.

—— (with Ronnie Mulryne and Margaret Shewring, eds), *The Design of the Globe*, London, 1993.

Harbage, Alfred N., *Annals of English Drama 975–1700*, Philadelphia, 1940; revised by S. Schoenbaum, 1964; 3rd edn Sylvia S. Wagenheim, New York, 1989.

——, *Shakespeare's Audience*, New York, 1941.

Hart, A, 'The Length of Elizabethan and Jacobean Plays', *Review of English Studies* 8 (1932) 139–54.

Hattaway, Michael, *Elizabethan Popular Theatre*, London and New York, 1982.

Heywood, Thomas, *The Four Prentices of London*, ed. Mary Ann Weber Gasior, New York and London, 1980.

Hildy, Franklin J, (ed.), *New Issues in the Reconstruction of Shakespeare's Theatre*, New York, 1991.

Hodges, C. Walter, *The Globe Restored*, London, 1963; 2nd edn, 1968.

Holinshed, Raphael, *The Chronicles of England, Scotlande and Irelande*, London, 1577.

——, *The First and Second Chronicles*, London, 1587.

Hosley, Richard, 'Shakespeare's Use of the Gallery over the Stage', *Shakespeare Survey* 10 (1957), 7–89.

——, 'The Discovery-Space in Shakespeare's Globe', *Shakespeare Survey* 12 (1959), 35–46.

——, 'Was there a Music-Room in Shakespeare's Globe?' *Shakespeare Survey* 13 (1960), 113–23.

Howard, Jean E., *Shakespeare's Art of Orchestration*, Urbana, 1984.

Hunter, G. K., 'Flatcaps and Bluecoats: Visual Signifiers on the Elizabethan Stage', *Essays and Studies* 33 (1980), 16–47.

Ichikawa, Mariko, 'A Note on Shakespeare's Stage Direction', *Shakespeare Studies* 22 (1983), 31–56.

——, 'Exits in Shakespeare's Plays: Time Allowed to Exiters', *Studies in English Literature*, 68 (Tokyo, 1992), 189–206.

Ingram, William, *The Business of Playing: the Beginnings of the Adult Professional Theater in Elizabethan London*, Ithaca and London, 1992.

Johnson, Samuel, *Selected Writings*, ed. Patrick Cruttwell, Harmondsworth, 1982.

Jonson, Ben, *Works*, 11 vols, eds C. H. Herford and Percy and Evelyn M. Simpson, Oxford, 1954 (first published 1925).

Kennan, Siobhan and Peter Davidson, 'The Icononography of the Bankside Globe', in *Shakespeare's Globe Rebuilt*, ed. J. R. Mulryne and Margaret Shewring, Cambridge, 1996.

Kiernan, Pauline, *Shakespeare's Theory Of Drama*, Cambridge, 1996 (repr. 1997; pb. 1998).

——, 'Findings from the Globe Workshop Season 1995', http//www.rdg.ac.uk/globe/Data-Base/Articles/Workshop.html.

——, 'Findings from the Globe Prologue Season', http//www.rdg.ac.uk/globe/Data-Base/Articles/Prologue.html.

——, 'A Report on the Opening Season at Shakespeare's Globe: *Henry V*', http//www.rdg.ac.uk/globe/ Data-Base / Articles / Opening Reports / Henry V.html.

King, T. J., *Shakespearean Staging 1599–1642*, Cambridge, Mass., 1971.

Kyd, Thomas, *The Spanish Tragedy*, ed. J. R. Mulryne, London, 1989.

Leggatt, Alexander, *Jacobean Public Theatre*, London and New York, 1992.

Leishman, J. B., *The Three Parnassus Plays*, London, 1949.

Lindenberger, Herbert, *Historical Drama: the Relation of Literature and Reality*, Chicago, 1975.

Lusardi, James, 'The Pictured Playhouse: Reading the Utrecht Engraving of Shakespeare's London,' *Shakespeare Quarterly* 44 (1993), 202–7.

Mann, David, *The Elizabethan Player*, London and New York, 1991.

Marston, John, *The Malcontent*, ed. G. K. Hunter, London, 1967.

Massinger, Philip, *The Plays and Poems*, ed. Philip Edwards and Colin Gibson, 5 vols, Oxford, 1976.

May, Robin, ed., *The Wit of the Theatre*, London, 1969.

Middleton, Thomas and Thomas Dekker, *The Roaring Girl*, ed. Elizabeth Cook, 2nd edn, London, 1997.

Middleton (?), Thomas, *Father Hubburd's Tale*, London, 1604.

Middleton, Thomas, *A Chaste Maid in Cheapside*, ed. Alan Brissenden, London, 1968.

Miller-Schutz, Chantal, 'A Report on the Opening Season at Shakespeare's Globe, *The Winter's Tale*' http//www.rdg.ac.uk/globe/DataBase/Articles/ OpeningReports/Winter.html.

Mulryne, J. R., and Margaret Shewring, eds, *Shakespeare's Globe Rebuilt*, Cambridge, 1997.

Murray, John Tucker, *English Dramatic Companies 1558–1642*, Vol. 1, 'London Companies', London, 1910.

Nashe, Thomas, *The Works*, 5 vols, ed. Ronald B. McKerrow; rev. F. P. Wilson, Oxford, 1966.

Nelsen, Paul, 'The Second Coming of the Globe: Will the Centre Hold?', *Shakespeare Bulletin*, Vol. 16, No. 1 (Winter 1998), 5–12.

——, 'The Heavens Must Wait: Fallout from "Workshop Season" Stymies Globe Progress', *Shakespeare Bulletin*, Vol. 13, No. 4 (Fall 1995), 37–8.

Nosworthy, J. M., '*Macbeth* at the Globe', *Library* 2 (1947), 108–18.

Orgel, Stephen, *Impersonations: the Performance of Gender in Shakespeare's England*, Cambridge, 1996.

Orrell, John, *The Quest for Shakespeare's Globe*, Cambridge, 1982.

——, 'Building the Fortune', *Shakespeare Quarterly* (1993), 127–44.

——, 'Beyond the Rose: Design Problems for the Globe Reconstruction', in *New Issues in the Reconstruction of Shakespeare's Theatre*, ed. Franklin J. Hildy, New York, 1990.

——, 'Sunlight at the Globe', *Theatre Notebook*, 38 (1984), 79–94.

——, 'Designing the Globe', in *Shakespeare's Globe Rebuilt*, ed. J. R. Mulryne and Margaret Shewring, Cambridge, 1997.

——, 'Reading the Documents', in *Shakespeare's Globe Rebuilt*, ed. J. R. Mulryne and Margaret Shewring, Cambridge, 1997.

——, *The Human Stage: English Theatre Design, 1567–1640*, Cambridge, 1988.

——, (with Andrew Gurr) *Rebuilding Shakespeare's Globe*, London, 1989.

Peat, Derek, 'Looking Back to Front: the View from the Lords' Room', in *Shakespeare and the Sense of Performance*, ed. Marvin and Ruth Thompson, Newark, 1989, 180–94.

Platter, Thomas, *Travels in England, 1599*, trans. Clare Williams, London, 1959.

Reynolds, George F, 'Was there a "Tarras" in Shakespeare's Globe?' *Shakespeare Survey* 4 (1951), 97–100.

——, '*Hamlet* at the Globe', *Shakespeare Survey* 9 (1956), 49–53.

Ringler, William A., Jr, 'The Number of Actors in Shakespeare's Early Plays', in *The Seventeenth-Century Stage*, ed. G. E. Bentley, Toronto, 1968.

Ronayne, John, '*Totus Mundus Agit Histrionem*. The Interior Decoration Scheme of the Bankside Globe', in *Shakespeare's Globe Rebuilt*, ed. J. R. Mulryne and Margaret Shewring, Cambridge, 1996.

Rozett Martha Tuck, *The Doctrine of Election and the Emergence of Elizabethan Tragedy*, Princeton, NJ, 1984.

Rutter, Carol Chillington, ed., *Documents of the Rose Playhouse*, Manchester, 1984.

Rylance, Mark, 'Playing the Globe: Artistic Policy and Practice', in *Shakespeare's Globe Rebuilt*, eds. J. R. Mulryne and Margaret Shewring, Cambridge, 1997.

Salgado, Gamini, *Eyewitnesses of Shakespeare: First-Hand Accounts of Performances 1590–1890*, Sussex, 1975.

Saunders, J. W., 'Staging at the Globe', *Shakespeare Quarterly* 11 (1960), 401–25.

Schanzer, Ernest, 'Thomas Platter's Observations on the Elizabethan Stage', *Notes and Queries* 201 (1956), 465–7.

Shakespeare, William, *The Complete Works*, ed. Stanley Wells and Gary Taylor, Oxford, 1986.

Shapiro, I. A., 'The Bankside Theatres: Early Engravings', *Shakespeare Survey* 1 (1948), 25–37.

——, 'An Original Drawing of the Globe Theatre', *Shakespeare Survey* 2 (1949), 21–3.

Shapiro, Michael, *Gender in Play on the Shakespearean Stage: Boy Heroines and Female Pages*, Ann Arbor, 1994.

——, 'Lady Wroth Describes a "Boy Actress"', *Medieval and Renaissance Drama in England*, Vol. 4, ed., J. Leeds Barroll, New York, 1987, pp. 187–94.

Shirley, Frances Ann, *Shakespeare's Use of Off-Stage Sounds*, Lincoln, Nebraska, 1963.

Skura, Meredith Ann, *Shakespeare's Actor and the Purposes of Playing*, Chicago, 1993.

Smallwood, Robert, 'Shakespeare Performances in England 1995–6', *Shakespeare Survey* 50 (1996). [Review of *The Two Gentlemen of Verona* in the Globe Prologue season]

Smith, Bruce R., *Homosexual Desire in Shakespeare's England*, Chicago and London, 1991.

Smith, Irwin, 'Theatre into Globe', *Shakespeare Quarterly* 3 (1952), 113–20.

——, 'Their Exits and Reentrances', *Shakespeare Quarterly* 18 (1967), 7–16.

Smith, Warren D., *Shakespeare's Playhouse Practice: a Handbook*, Hanover, New Hampshire, 1975.

——, 'Evidence of Scaffolding on Shakespeare's Stage', *Review of English Studies* n.s. 2 (1951) 22–9.

Sprinchorn, Evert, 'An Intermediate Stage Level in the Elizabethan Theatre', *Theatre Notebook*, 46 (1992), 73–94.

Streett, J. B., 'The Durability of Boy Actors', *Notes and Queries* 218 (1973), 461–3.

Stubbes, Phillip, *The Anatomie of Abuses*, ed. F. J. Furnival, London, 1887–89.

Styan, J. L., *Shakespeare's Stagecraft*, Cambridge, 1967.

Thompson, Marvin and Ruth, eds, *Shakespeare and the Sense of Performance*, Newark, 1989.

Thomson, Peter, *Shakespeare's Theatre*, London, 1985.

Tourneur, Cyril, *The Atheist's Tragedy*, in *Jacobean Tragedies*, ed. A. H. Gomme, Oxford, 1969.

Walsh, John, 'What's This? Punch and Judy at the Globe? As Shakespeare Goes Interactive, It's Time the Audience Learnt its Lines', *The Independent*, 29 August 1996. [Review of *The Two Gentlemen of Verona*]

Weaver, Maurice, 'Rowdiness at the Globe "would be bad for the Bard"', *The Telegraph*, 28 August 1996.

Webster, John, *The White Devil*, ed. John Russell Brown, London, 1960.

Weever, John, *The Mirror of Martyrs*, London, 1601.

Weimann, Robert, *Shakespeare and the Popular Tradition in the Theatre*, ed. and trans. Robert Schwartz, London, 1978.

White, Beatrice, *An Index to the 'Elizabethan Stage' and 'William Shakespeare: a Study of Facts and Problems' by Sir Edmund Chambers*, Oxford, 1934.

Wickham, Glynne, *Early English Stages, 1300–1660*, 4 vols, London, 1959–.

——, *Shakespeare's Dramatic Heritage*, London 1969.

——, '"Heavens", Machinery, and Pillars in the Theatre and Other Early Playhouses' in *The First Public Playhouse: the Theatre in Shoreditch 1576–1598*, ed. Herbert Berry, Montreal, 1979, 1–15.

Wiles, David, *Shakespeare's Clown: Actor and Text in the Elizabethan Playhouse,* Cambridge, 1987.

Worthen, W. B., *Shakespeare and the Authority of Performance* (Cambridge, 1997).

Zitner, Sheldon P., 'Gosson, Ovid, and the Elizabethan Audience', *Shakespeare Quarterly* 9 (1958), 206–8.

Index